Athlone French Poets

VERLAINE

Athlone French Poets

General Editor: EILEEN LE BRETON
*Reader in French Language and Literature,
Bedford College, University of London*

MONOGRAPHS

Verlaine *by C. Chadwick*

Gérard de Nerval *by Norma Rinsler*

Saint-John Perse *by Roger Little*

CRITICAL EDITIONS

Paul Valéry: Charmes ou Poèmes
edited by Charles G. Whiting

Paul Verlaine: Sagesse
edited by C. Chadwick

Gérard de Nerval: Les Chimères
edited by Norma Rinsler

Saint-John Perse: Exil
edited by Roger Little

VERLAINE

by

C. CHADWICK

UNIVERSITY OF LONDON
THE ATHLONE PRESS
1973

Published by
THE ATHLONE PRESS
UNIVERSITY OF LONDON
at 4 Gower Street, London WC1

Distributed by
Tiptree Book Services Ltd
Tiptree, Essex

U.S.A. and Canada
Humanities Press Inc
New York

0 485 14603 7 *cloth*
0 485 12203 0 *paperback*

Printed in Great Britain by
The Garden City Press Limited
Letchworth, Hertfordshire
SG6 1JS

Athlone French Poets

General Editor EILEEN LE BRETON

This series is designed to provide students and general readers both with Monographs on important nineteenth- and twentieth-century French poets and Critical Editions of representative works by these poets.

The Monographs aim at presenting the essential biographical facts while placing the poet in his social and intellectual context. They contain a detailed analysis of his poetical works and, where appropriate, a brief account of his other writings. His literary reputation is examined and his contribution to the development of French poetry is assessed, as is also his impact on other literatures. A selection of critical views and a bibliography are appended.

The critical Editions contain a substantial introduction aimed at presenting each work against its historical background as well as studying its genre, structure, themes, style, etc. and highlighting its relevance for today. The text normally given is the complete text of the original edition. It is followed by full commentaries on the poems and annotation of the text, including variant readings when these are of real significance, and a select bibliography.

E. Le B.

PREFACE

Although Verlaine's colourful life has been studied by a number of writers, ranging from his friend Edmond Lepelletier in 1907 to Joanna Richardson in 1971, his work has attracted much less attention, especially among English critics who have tended to treat it as almost incidental to his life. The purpose of the present volume is to redress the balance by restricting biographical details to a short opening chapter and devoting the remaining chapters to Verlaine's poetry and prose. Any such study is inevitably indebted to the work of those French critics who have helped to maintain the reputation of Verlaine as a writer. Among these special mention must be made of Pierre Martino whose *Verlaine*, first published in 1924, remained, for almost thirty years, virtually the only book on the poet rather than the man. In 1953 a renewal of interest in this aspect of Verlaine began with Antoine Adam's persuasive study of the early poetry and his rather less convincing attempt to rescue from oblivion the later verse. This was followed by a succession of critical studies, notably by J. H. Bornecque, Claude Cuénot, Octave Nadal, Georges Zayed and Eléonore Zimmermann, which were accompanied by much improved editions of Verlaine's work, thanks to the labours of Y. G. Le Dantec, Jacques Robichez, Jacques Borel and Henri de Bouillane de Lacoste. The task of reconciling the sometimes conflicting views of these and other critics has not always been an easy one and it has, on occasions, been rendered even more difficult by the author's inability to resist the temptation to advance his own ideas. It is hoped, nevertheless, that a balanced assessment of Verlaine's achievement has been reached and that the aim of the series of which this volume forms part has thus been fulfilled.

The University, Aberdeen   C. C.

CONTENTS

to *N O'B*

THE BIOGRAPHICAL BACKGROUND

From his very earliest years, by what is perhaps no more than a curious coincidence, Paul-Marie Verlaine led the unsettled existence that was to be the distinctive hallmark of the rest of his life. His father was an army officer garrisoned at Metz in eastern France at the time of Verlaine's birth on 30 March 1844. He was then posted to Montpellier in the south of France the following year and he and his wife and child moved twice more, to the nearby towns of Sète and Nîmes, before they returned to Metz early in 1849. Two years later Captain Verlaine resigned his commission at the age of fifty and the family moved to Paris.

Circumstances also led to Verlaine, in his early years, being a spoilt child, and here too it is a curious and perhaps significant fact that a certain wilfulness and emotional immaturity remained with him for the rest of his life. He was an only child and was, furthermore, a long-awaited child, since his mother had been married for thirteen years, during which she had suffered three miscarriages, before Verlaine was born. It is, in consequence, scarcely surprising that she should have doted on him and her attitude was shared by her niece, Elisa Moncomble, eight years older than Verlaine, who had been orphaned and whom Mme Verlaine brought up as an elder sister to her son. There seems every likelihood too that he was spoilt on other occasions in that both his parents maintained close links with the families to which they belonged and Verlaine spent frequent holidays either with his father's relatives at Paliseul and Jehonville in Belgian Luxembourg, or with his mother's relatives at Fampoux near Arras.

It was no doubt because of this atmosphere of indulgence in which he was brought up that Verlaine made little or no attempt to achieve any creditable results at school and in the months he spent at University in 1862 and 1863 he continued farther along the same path, spending more time drinking in the cafés of the Latin Quarter than in studying law. His father's insistence in 1864 that he should take a job as a clerk, at first in an insurance company and later in the Hôtel de Ville, scarcely altered his Bohemian way of life and with the death of his father in December 1865 the last restraint that might have held Verlaine's wilful and wayward behaviour in check was removed.

But although he may have become increasingly unstable in character Verlaine had also begun to express his thoughts and feelings in poetry and after having a few poems and articles accepted by magazines he published his first volume of verse, *Poèmes saturniens*, towards the end of 1866, the money for its publication being provided by Elisa Moncomble, or Madame Dujardin as she had become since her marriage in 1861. This was, however, to be her last act of kindness towards her cousin since she died in childbirth a few months afterwards. Her death was a profound shock to Verlaine, as was that of another close relative two years later, the aunt at Paliseul with whom he had spent so many holidays. On both occasions his grief took the outward form of one of the heavy bouts of drinking which were becoming increasingly frequent with him and which, it has been suggested, may have marked the re-appearance in him, a generation later, of a tendency to alchoholism which is known to have affected his paternal grandfather.

It may well be that by the time he was twenty-five Verlaine himself realised that it was imperative for him to introduce some kind of stability into his life by marrying, though his choice of Mathilde Mauté, a girl of sixteen, almost ten years younger than himself, seems, in the circumstances, an unwise one. At first, however, Mathilde undoubtedly gave to Verlaine's life that sense of direction in which, until then, it had been singularly lacking, so that the volume of verse that he wrote for her during their engagement in the last half of 1869 and the first half of 1870, *La Bonne Chanson*, is very different in tone from the volume which had preceded it, *Fêtes galantes*, published early in 1869.

It is perhaps conceivable that Mathilde would have continued to exercise this salutary effect on Verlaine's character after their marriage in August 1870 had it not been for the political events of the time. The Franco-Prussian war had just broken out and it was brought to a virtual end the following month with the crushing defeat of the French at Sedan. During the ensuing siege of Paris Verlaine was a member of the National Guard and when a state of civil war came into existence in Paris after the armistice of January 1871, he was on the side of the rebellious Commune which was finally defeated by the legitimate forces of the Versaillais in May 1871. He discreetly left Paris the following month for fear of reprisals, taking Mathilde with him to his relatives at Fampoux, and on his return to the capital in August he felt it wiser to lie low rather than to draw attention to himself by trying to get back his old job as a municipal government employee. These twelve months of turmoil imposed an intolerable strain on the marriage and by September 1871 there is no doubt that Verlaine was once more in that state of instability from which Mathilde had temporarily rescued him.

It was just about at this time that he received a letter from Charleville, near the Franco-Belgian frontier and no more than twenty miles from Paliseul and Jehonville, written by a young poet ten years his junior, Arthur Rimbaud, who pleaded for help in his desperate anxiety to escape from his provincial backwater and to get to Paris. Verlaine, without a job, living with his parents-in-law and no doubt finding it difficult to bear with the fact that Mathilde was eight months pregnant, must have regarded this as a golden opportunity to give some point to life and he promptly invited Rimbaud to come and stay at the Mautés' house in Paris. Rimbaud soon made himself so unpleasant to his hosts that he had to go and live elsewhere, but Verlaine refused to tolerate any criticism of his new friend. The consequent arguments on this point between Mathilde and her husband rose to such a pitch of violence that in January 1872 M. Mauté took his daughter and her two months old son away from Paris and from then until their return in the middle of March Verlaine lived with Rimbaud.

There is no doubt that owing, it may be presumed, to the circumstances of his childhood and to the largely feminine atmosphere in which he had been brought up, Verlaine had a homosexual side to his character. Throughout his life he formed close associations with a succession of men—Lucien Viotti while still at school, then Rimbaud in 1872 and 1873, Lucien Létinois a few years later and in the last decade of his life Frédéric-Auguste Cazals. Rimbaud too, again owing, presumably, to the circumstances of his childhood, had homosexual tendencies, though in his case it was probably lack of maternal affection which caused his revulsion against women, whereas Verlaine seems, on the contrary, to have wanted a strong personality to provide him with some stability. In this sense therefore Rimbaud and Verlaine were complementary to each other and the letters and poems written during these first months of their relationship leave no room for argument about the fact that extremely strong emotional ties existed between them. 'Aime-moi, protège et donne confiance. Etant très faible, j'ai très besoin de bontés', wrote Verlaine in a letter dated 2 April 1872, and another letter written about a month later ended with the words: 'Maintenant, salut, revoir, joie, attente de lettres, attente de Toi. Moi avoir deux fois cette nuit rêvé: Toi, martyriseur d'enfant . . .'[1] Yet, in a typically indecisive way, Verlaine could not bring himself to abandon his wife completely. When Mathilde had returned to Paris in the middle of March 1872 Rimbaud had gone back to Charleville to enable the couple to patch up their marriage, but before the end of May Verlaine brought Rimbaud back to Paris again and the difficulties between husband and wife soon recurred. On 7 July Verlaine seemed to have at last made up his mind since he left Paris with Rimbaud and headed for Belgium. From Brussels however he wrote to his wife in the most plaintive terms: 'Ma pauvre Mathilde, n'aie pas de chagrin, ne pleure pas, je fais un mauvais rêve, je reviendrai un jour',[2] and towards the end of July Mathilde set off for Brussels where she persuaded Verlaine to come back to Paris with her. Or at least she persuaded him to get on the train to Paris with her, but at the Franco-Belgian frontier he suddenly left the train and went back to Brussels to rejoin Rimbaud.

After another month in Belgium the two poets crossed the Channel on 7 September and settled in London but the 'époux infernal' soon tired of the 'vierge folle', to use Rimbaud's terms. Before the end of the year he returned to Charleville, leaving Verlaine alone in London, and although he went back there in January 1873 because Verlaine had fallen ill, both of them left London early in April, Verlaine going to Jehonville and Rimbaud to Charleville or, strictly speaking, to the family farm at Roche a few miles away where he began *Une Saison en Enfer*. Although the fact that Rimbaud had begun this work, which is essentially one of disillusionment, would seem to suggest that the relationship between him and Verlaine was at an end, the two poets did make one last attempt to come together again, on Verlaine's initiative. 'Pour l'instant, je t'embrasse bien et compte sur une bien prochaine entrevue, dont tu me donnes l'espoir pour cette semaine. Dès que tu me feras signe, j'y serai',[3] wrote Verlaine on 18 May and after meeting at Bouillon, halfway between Roche and Jehonville, a few days later, they left once again for London. But after little more than a month yet another of the violent quarrels with which their relationship was increasingly punctuated flared up and Verlaine rushed off to Brussels on 3 July threatening to commit suicide unless he could effect a reconciliation with his wife. On the cross-channel steamer Verlaine wrote to Rimbaud: 'Tu dois, au fond, comprendre, enfin, qu'il me fallait absolument partir, que cette vie violente et toute de scènes sans motif que ta fantaisie ne pouvait m'aller foutre plus . . . Si d'ici à trois jours, je ne suis par r'avec ma femme, dans des conditions parfaites, je me brûle la gueule'.[4] Not surprisingly, his wife made no response to his appeal to her, but his mother, on the other hand, hurried to Brussels in answer to his message to her, as did Rimbaud to whom he sent a telegram on 8 July reading: 'Volontaire Espagne. Viens ici, hôtel Liégeois. Blanchisseuse, manuscrits, si possible'.[5] The intention of committing suicide had therefore quickly faded to be replaced by the slightly less flamboyant gesture of going off to join in the fighting that had broken out in the newly proclaimed Spanish Republic. But this dream of death or glory also faded very rapidly and when Rimbaud arrived Verlaine insisted that they should pick up the threads of their relationship once more. But Rimbaud adamantly refused to do this, despite Verlaine's pleas, and on 10 July the latter's wildly erratic behaviour and obvious mental instability came to a climax. He bought a revolver and fired two shots at Rimbaud in their hotel room, hitting him in the wrist. Typically, he was immediately filled with remorse for what he had done and took Rimbaud to hospital to have his wound attended to. Later that same day however, on the way to the railway station, since Rimbaud persisted in his intention of leaving Verlaine, the latter made a move to pull out his revolver again, or at least appeared to do so to Rimbaud who called a nearby policeman for help and Verlaine was arrested.

Although Rimbaud, in a statement he made to the police on 19 July tried to have the charges dropped,[6] Verlaine nevertheless had to stand trial and on 8 August was condemned to two years' imprisonment, a relatively heavy penalty that was due to the prejudice felt against him because of his relationship with Rimbaud. He appealed against the sentence but on 27 August it was confirmed and two months later he was transferred from the prison in Brussels to the prison at Mons for the remainder of his sentence.

Verlaine had already put together his fourth volume of verse, *Romances sans Paroles*, some three or four months before and during his early days in prison he was busy arranging for its publication. But he soon had plans for a fifth volume of verse to be entitled *Cellulairement* which, as the title suggests, was to be made up of the fairly substantial amount of verse that he wrote in prison. But before he had served half his sentence an event occurred, or rather two related events, which were ultimately to lead to the abandonment of this project. However extraordinary it may seem, Verlaine still cherished hopes of being reconciled with his wife, but at the beginning of May 1874 the news was brought to him that Mathilde had finally been successful in obtaining a legal separation from him. He was once more therefore plunged into that state of instability and uncertainty from which he seems to have spent his life trying desperately hard to escape in various ways. Immediately after receiving news of the separation he asked to see the prison chaplain and expressed a wish to return to the Catholic faith in which he had been brought up but from which he had tended to drift away in the intervening years. After some weeks of religious instruction Verlaine announced his conversion to the chaplain in June and on 15 August the latter allowed him to take communion.

Verlaine's conversion was at first a purely emotional experience and while he remained in prison, sheltered from the temptations of the outside world, his faith continued to be of this kind. But he had in fact only a few more months' imprisonment to serve since he was granted a substantial reduction of his sentence, and after he emerged from prison on 16 January 1875 he realised that he needed to take practical steps to defend his new-found faith. It is no doubt this that explains his departure in March for England where he took up a teaching post in the quiet village of Stickney in Lincolnshire. There he led an orderly life for twelve months, interrupted only by equally orderly holiday periods with his mother in Arras. During this time his reflections on his conversion and his determination to resist temptation inspired a number of religious poems which he decided to add to some of the more sombre poems of *Cellulairement* with a view to constituting a new and less hetero-geneous volume of verse to be called *Sagesse*.

In September 1876, after an unsuccessful attempt to set up as a private teacher of French in the town of Boston, a few miles away from Stickney, Verlaine left Lincolnshire for the south of England to take up another post at a school in Bournemouth. This lasted for twelve months before he returned to France in September 1877 to take up a teaching post, until July 1879, at Rethel in the north-eastern part of France that he knew so well. During these three years Verlaine continued to add to the poems of *Sagesse*, although his themes were no longer solely religious and included numerous landscapes, four appeals to Mathilde, written in 1878 in yet another attempt at reconciliation, and a few poems with a political flavour, his fervent return to the Catholic faith having been accompanied by an equally fervent rejection of his former republican opinions.

By the time *Sagesse* was published however, in December 1880 although it bears the date 1881, Verlaine had already begun to fall from grace. When he had first gone to Rethel he had become deeply attached to one of his pupils, Lucien Létinois, and had also resumed his drinking habits. It was for these reasons that his teaching post at Rethel was not renewed after July 1879 and he left for England with Létinois, who took over Verlaine's former post at Stickney while Verlaine himself took a teaching job at Lymington, near Bournemouth. But after three months both of them flung up their posts and returned to France where Verlaine, suddenly inspired by the thought of at last finding a haven of peace in the countryside, bought a farm at Juniville just south of Rethel and settled there in March 1880 with Létinois and the latter's parents. But either through his own idleness or that of the Létinois, Verlaine's farming exploit was a financial disaster and two years later, at the beginning of 1882 the farm had to be sold at a considerable loss.

After the failure of this attempt at country life Verlaine returned to Paris, still accompanied by the Létinois family, and tried to get himself re-instated in his old job at the Hôtel de Ville that he had left twelve years before. Here too he met with failure and suffered an even worse blow with the death from typhoid fever on 7 April 1883 of Lucien Létinois who had been his constant companion for six years. But these unhappy episodes in Verlaine's life at this period were counterbalanced by his re-entry into the literary world. *Sagesse* had made, it is true, no very great impression in 1881, but the publication in 1882 of the poem 'Art poétique', written eight years before, attracted some attention and from 1883 to 1886 a series of essays entitled *Les Poètes maudits*, first published in the magazines *Lutèce* and *La Vogue* and later in volume form, finally made of Verlaine a writer of considerable repute.

By then however, still pursuing his erratic existence, Verlaine had left Paris once more and, despite the lesson of Juniville, had bought from the parents of the dead Lucien their farm at Coulommes near Rethel where he went to live with his mother in September 1883. For the next eighteen months he led a life of utter debauchery, as if he had finally given way to the tendencies he had tried hard to hold in check, with increasing difficulty, for the last ten years. His drunkenness was legendary in the district and on more than one occasion he treated his mother with a brutality that can only be explained by the fact that he had completely lost control of himself. One of these attacks led to his being condemned, in the spring of 1885, to a month's imprisonment and a fine of 500 francs which he managed to pay out of the proceeds of the sale of the farm at Coulommes shortly before, for which he received little more than half what had been paid for it by Madame Verlaine who, doting as ever, had made it over to her son.

When Verlaine gave up this second attempt at living in the peace of the countryside and returned to live in Paris in June 1885 his financial affairs were in a sorry state and it is from this time that the last lamentable period in his life begins during which 'le pauvre Lélian', as he had called himself in *Les Poètes maudits*, was always on the verge of destitution. What little money he and his mother possessed—it goes without saying that Madame Verlaine, in spite of everything, came to live with him in Paris—finally disappeared when the latter died on 21 January 1886. The Mauté family claimed the remnants of her fortune on the grounds that Verlaine had failed to comply with a court order to contribute to the upkeep of his son. The money Verlaine earned from his writing he immediately spent and he relied upon help, in cash and in kind, from his circle of friends to keep his creditors at bay. In 1894 fifteen friends, led by the novelist Maurice Barrès and the dilettante Comte Robert de Montes-quiou, formed a committee of subscribers to offer regular aid to him and this was supplemented by a succession of grants from the government.

In addition to his desperate financial plight, Verlaine's health rapidly deteriorated. A painful form of rheumatism in his knee had prevented him from attending his mother's funeral and six months later he spent a month in hospital, to be quickly followed by a much longer spell of over four months from early November 1886 to mid March 1887. From then until his death in January 1896 Verlaine spent most of his time in hospital,[7] emerging for brief spells during which he continued to lead the sordid exis-tence into which he had now permanently sunk, spending much of his time drinking in the cafés of the Latin Quarter and living in disreputable hotels or rented rooms with one or other of the two women, Eugénie Krantz and Philomène Boudin, with whom he shared the last half-dozen years of his life.

Yet paradoxically, although this was a period of persistent illness, constant poverty and endless debauchery for Verlaine, it was also the period when his place as a major literary figure was at last fully recognised. From 1885 to 1893 he contributed some thirty articles on contemporary authors to a periodical publi-cation entitled *Les Hommes d'aujourd'hui*. He was invited to make a lecture tour of Holland in November 1892, of Belgium in February and March 1893 and of England in November and December 1893. In the summer of 1893 he put his name forward as a candidate for the French Academy, without any success, but in August 1894, on the death of Leconte de Lisle, he was elected to the less formal position of Prince of Poets, receiving twice as many votes as his nearest rivals, Heredia and Mallarmé. A further paradox however is that he was in fact no longer a poet of any real talent and, with few, if any, exceptions, the vast number of verses he turned out during the last ten years of his life are worthless. *Jadis et Naguère*, which he had published in 1884, is made up, as the title suggests, of poems composed some time before, several of the most powerful having been taken from the abandoned *Cellulairement* and written therefore some ten years earlier. It was not until 1888 that Verlaine published a volume of recently composed verse. This was *Amour* which he intended as a sequel or companion volume to *Sagesse* and which was followed three years later by another volume of the same high moral tone, *Bonheur*, in 1891 and in 1892 by *Liturgies intimes* whose religious note is evident from the title.

It may appear yet another paradox that Verlaine should have been writing this kind of poetry when the life he was then leading was in such startling contrast to it. But this may be explained by the fact that his spiritual aspirations continued to exist although he was by then quite incapable of giving them any practical form. A less charitable explanation however could be that Verlaine was well aware of the fact that his reputation rested in a large measure on *Sagesse* and that he was anxious to maintain his image as a religious poet. At the same time he was equally well aware that the public found something fascinating in the extraordinary duality of his character and he did not hesitate therefore to complete his self-portrait of a fallen angel by publishing, parallel with his other verse, volumes concerned not with the spirit but with the flesh. The first of these volumes was in fact entitled *Parallèlement* and was published in 1889 at the same time as the second edition of *Sagesse*. In 1891, parallel with *Bonheur*, he published *Chansons pour Elle*, inspired largely by Eugénie Krantz whose praises he also sang in *Odes en son Honneur* in 1893, the year after the publication of *Liturgies intimes*. At the same time her rival, Philomène Boudin, was the muse whose doubtful virtues he celebrated in two volumes, one bearing the surprising title *Elégies* in 1893 and another one much more appropriately entitled *Dans les Limbes* in 1894. Finally, in 1896, the year of his death, *Chair* was published, inspired, as one critic has put it, 'par Philomène Boudin et Eugénie Krantz tour à tour et sans doute aussi par quelques autres "chères amies" '.[8]

A third vein which Verlaine readily exploited during these years of fame and years of decline was that of occasional verse and he published three volumes of this kind, *Dédicaces* in 1890, *Epigrammes* in 1894 and *Invectives* in 1896. Yet a fourth vein was that of his memoirs, and *Mes Hôpitaux* in 1891 was followed by *Mes Prisons* in 1893 and by *Confessions* in 1895, though an earlier volume, *Mémoires d'un Veuf*, published in 1886, despite its title, is more like a collection of short stories and was accompanied in the same year by three other short stories and a playlet under the general title of the longest of the stories, *Louise Leclercq*.

Extensive though this list may be it by no means covers all of Verlaine's large and varied output during the last years of his life. There were two volumes of obscene poems published clandestinely, *Femmes*, in 1891 and a companion volume, *Hombres*, in 1903 after Verlaine's death. The year 1903 also saw the publication of *Œuvres posthumes* whilst a short collection entitled *Biblio-sonnets* appeared in 1913 and two volumes under the title *Œuvres oubliées* in 1926 and 1929. These however do little or nothing to alter the image of Verlaine as a poet who reached his zenith in and around the year 1873 just before he reached the age of thirty. From then on his talent was on the wane, descending increasingly steeply towards its nadir marked by his death on 8 January 1896.

II

THE EARLY POETRY

Poèmes saturniens

Verlaine's first volume of poetry, *Poèmes saturniens*, appeared to-wards the end of 1866. At that time he was only twenty-two years old and it is therefore scarcely surprising that he should have been strongly influenced by the Parnassian poets then in vogue under the leadership of Leconte de Lisle who had published his *Poèmes antiques* in 1852 and his *Poèmes barbares* in 1862. The 'Prologue' and the 'Epilogue' to the *Poèmes saturniens* in fact preach in emphatic terms the principles of the Parnassian movement—that poets must remain 'au-dessus de la mêlée', con-cerned only with beauty:

> C'est qu'ils ont à la fin compris qu'il ne faut plus
> Mêler leur note pure aux cris irrésolus
> Que va poussant la foule obscène et violente,
> Et que l'isolement sied à leur marche lente.
> Le Poète, l'amour du Beau, voilà sa foi . . .

Furthermore, poetry is the fruit, not of sudden inspiration but of patient industry and, as Théophile Gautier had declared in his *Emaux et Camées*, is analogous to sculpture in that it must be slowly and carefully shaped:

> Libre à nos Inspirés, cœurs qu'une œillade emflamme,
> D'abandonner leur être aux vents comme un bouleau;
> Pauvres gens! l'Art n'est pas d'éparpiller son âme:
> Est-elle en marbre, ou non, la Vénus de Milo?
>
> Nous donc, sculptons avec le ciseau des Pensées
> Le bloc vierge du Beau . . .[1]

The suggestion made by one critic that these lines are to be read ironically and that Verlaine is in fact mocking the Parnassian aesthetic[2] seems difficult to accept in view of the fact that he not only preaches the principles of the Parnassians but also puts into practice some of the more obvious features of their poetry, such as a tendency to use the Greek forms of proper names, as in the 'Prologue':

> Homéros, s'il n'a pas, lui, manié le glaive,
> Fait retentir, clameur immense qui s'élève,
> Vos échos jamais las, vastes postérités,
> D'Hektôr, et d'Odysseus, et d'Akhilleus chantés . . .

and to use terms from Indian mythology, again as in the 'Prologue':

> Une connexité grandiosement alme
> Liait le Kchatrya serein au Chanteur calme,
> Valmiki l'excellent à l'excellent Rama . . .

In some of the poems, however, such as 'La Mort de Philippe II', Verlaine no doubt owes as much to the Victor Hugo of *La Légende des Siècles*, the first volume of which had been published in 1859, as he does to Leconte de Lisle, and in a considerable number he is obviously indebted to Baudelaire whose *Fleurs du Mal* had first appeared in 1857. The very title of *Poèmes saturniens* is, in all probability, borrowed from Baudelaire's 'Epigraphe pour un livre condamné' in which he describes *Les Fleurs du Mal* as a 'livre saturnien', and such poems as 'Lassitude', 'Sérénade' and the second of the two poems entitled 'Nevermore' are strongly influenced by Baudelaire. Both the title of the sonnet 'Lassitude' and its theme of 'Calme un peu ces transports fébriles, ma charmante', are reminiscent of Baudelaire's 'Sed non satiata' with its appeal: 'O démon sans pitié! verse-moi moins de flamme'. 'Sérénade' is pure Baudelaire, in the third stanza in particular:

> Je chanterai tes yeux d'or et d'onyx
>   Purs de toutes ombres,
> Puis le Léthé de ton sein, puis le Styx
>   De tes cheveux sombres . . .

and it uses the same complicated pattern of refrains as Baudelaire's 'Le Beau Navire', in which, after the three opening stanzas, the first stanza is repeated, then, after a further two stanzas, the second stanza is repeated, and finally, after a further two stanzas, the third stanza is repeated. The only difference is that Verlaine, typically, gives up at the second stage and fails to carry the pattern through to completion. 'Nevermore' adopts another Baudelairian device, used in 'Le Balcon', 'Reversibilité', 'L'Irréparable' and 'Moesta et Errabunda', of repeating the first line of each stanza as the last line, and in places the vocabulary and the stately rhythm are Baudelairian in the extreme:

> Le Bonheur a marché côte à côte avec moi;
> Mais la Fatalité ne connaît point de trêve:
> Le ver est dans le fruit, le réveil dans le rêve,
> Et le remords est dans l'amour: telle est la loi,
> — Le Bonheur a marché côte à côte avec moi.

But alongside such derivative poetry can be found a good many poems which, even at this early stage, have a distinctly original flavour. 'Soleils couchants', for example, may owe something to Baudelaire's poetry, and especially perhaps to his 'Harmonie du Soir' in that both make use of a landscape to evoke a mood, both employ a limited number of rhymes and both engage in a considerable amount of repetition. But 'Harmonie du Soir' has the slow and regular rhythm so typical of Baudelaire:

> Voici venir les temps où vibrant sur sa tige
> Chaque fleur s'évapore ainsi qu'un encensoir;
> Les sons et les parfums tournent dans l'air du soir;
> Valse mélancolique et langoureux vertige!
>
> Chaque fleur s'évapore ainsi qu'un encensoir;
> Le violon frémit comme un cœur qu'on afflige;
> Valse mélancolique et langoureux vertige!
> Le ciel est triste et beau comme un grand reposoir . . .

'Soleils couchants' in contrast has a quicker, hesitant rhythm, with the repetitions irregularly placed and with 'enjambement' the rule rather than the exception, so that the poem has that air of spontaneity, that intimate rather than oratorical note that was to become the outstandingly original feature of Verlaine's poetry:

> Une aube affaiblie
> Verse par les champs
> La mélancolie
> Des soleils couchants.
> La mélancolie
> Berce de doux chants
> Mon cœur qui s'oublie
> Aux soleils couchants.
> Et d'étranges rêves,
> Comme des soleils
> Couchants sur les grèves,
> Fantômes vermeils,
> Défilent sans trêves,
> Défilent, pareils
> A de grands soleils
> Couchants sur les grèves.

'Crépuscule du Soir mystique' also seems to owe something to 'Harmonie du Soir', not only by its title but by a similar use of no more than two rhymes throughout the poem and by a similar theme and similar vocabulary. But again Baudelaire's highly complex system of regularly repeated lines, creating a solemn and stately tone, is replaced in Verlaine's poem by a single sentence made up of a series of subordinate clauses strung one after the other in a seemingly casual way:

> Le Souvenir avec le Crépuscule
> Rougeoie et tremble à l'ardent horizon
> De l'Espérance en flamme qui recule
> Et s'agrandit ainsi qu'une cloison
> Mystérieuse où mainte floraison
> — Dahlia, lys, tulipe et renoncule—
> S'élance autour d'un treillis, et circule
> Parmi la maladive exhalaison
> De parfums lourds et chauds, dont le poison
> — Dahlia, lys, tulipe et renoncule—
> Noyant mes sens, mon âme et ma raison,
> Mêle dans une immense pâmoison
> Le Souvenir avec le Crépuscule.

'Le Rossignol' too is made up of a single flowing sentence covering twenty lines in the course of which Verlaine repeats the verb 's'abattre' and the expression 'plus rien' three times and adds one clause after another in an apparently spontaneous fashion:

> Comme un vol criard d'oiseaux en émoi,
> Tous mes souvenirs s'abattent sur moi,
> S'abattent parmi le feuillage jaune
> De mon cœur mirant son tronc plié d'aune
> Au tain violet de l'eau des Regrets
> Qui mélancoliquement coule auprès,
> S'abattent, et puis la rumeur mauvaise
> Qu'une brise moite en montant apaise,
> S'éteint par degrés dans l'arbre, si bien
> Qu'au bout d'un instant on n'entend plus rien,
> Plus rien que la voix célébrant l'Absente,
> Plus rien que la voix—ô si languissante!—
> De l'oiseau que fut mon Premier Amour,
> Et qui chante encor comme au premier jour;
> Et, dans la splendeur triste d'une lune

Se levant blafarde et solennelle, une
Nuit mélancolique et lourde d'été,
Pleine de silence et d'obscurité,
Berce sur l'azur qu'un vent doux effleure
L'arbre qui frissonne et l'oiseau qui pleure.

Similarly in 'Promenade sentimentale' there are long sinuous sentences and irregular repetitions with the first line re-appearing in altered form in lines thirteen and fourteen, while the last two lines use the vocabulary of the third and fourth lines but marshal the words in a slightly different order, and the phrases 'promenant ma plaie' and 'parmi la saulaie' which are at the end of lines five and six are switched to the beginning of lines eleven and twelve. All this takes away any rhetorical, declamatory effect and yet the point the poet wishes to make is still insidiously driven home to the reader; Baudelaire's insistent refrains have become tenuous and uncertain echoes which are nevertheless equally effective:

Le couchant dardait ses rayons suprêmes
Et le vent berçait les nénuphars blêmes;
Les grands nénuphars entre les roseaux
Tristement luisaient sur les calmes eaux.
Moi j'errais tout seul, promenant ma plaie
Au long de l'étang, parmi la saulaie
Où la brume vague évoquait un grand
Fantôme laiteux se désespérant
Et pleurant avec la voix des sarcelles
Qui se rappelaient en battant des ailes
Parmi la saulaie où j'errais tout seul
Promenant ma plaie; et l'épais linceul
Des ténèbres vint noyer les suprêmes
Rayons du couchant dans ses ondes blêmes
Et des nénuphars, parmi les roseaux,
Des grands nénuphars sur les calmes eaux.

In these and other *Paysages tristes*, as they are collectively sub-titled, Verlaine avoids using the twelve-syllable alexandrine, save on one occasion, preferring instead the less grandiose rhythm of the ten-syllable line in 'Crépuscule du Soir mystique', 'Le Rossignol', 'Promenade sentimentale' and 'L'Heure du Berger' while 'Chanson d'Automne' and 'Soleils couchants' have the even shorter and more fleeting rhythms of three- and four-syllable lines in the one case and five-syllable lines in the other.

These two poems also mark the introduction into Verlaine's poetry of the 'vers impair', the line with an uneven number of syllables. This was to become a feature of Verlaine's poetry, so much so that in the opening verse of his 'Art poétique' he was to urge the use of the 'vers impair' as being

> Plus vague et plus soluble dans l'air
> Sans rien en lui qui pèse ou qui pose.

This is because the reader's ear, attuned to lines with even numbers of syllables, expects an extra syllable at the end of the line and so hurries on to the following line, thus further adding to the 'uncomposed', casual quality of Verlaine's poetry. But even when using the alexandrine, as in 'Mon Rêve familier', Verlaine can still succeed in creating an almost conversational tone by means of hesitations and repetitions which convey the impression that he is thinking aloud and engaging in a kind of intimate confession:

> Je fais souvent ce rêve étrange et pénétrant
> D'une femme inconnue, et que j'aime, et qui m'aime,
> Et qui n'est, chaque fois, ni tout à fait la même
> Ni tout à fait une autre, et m'aime et me comprend.
>
> Car elle me comprend, et mon cœur, transparent
> Pour elle seule, hélas! cesse d'être un problème
> Pour elle seule, et les moiteurs de mon front blême,
> Elle seule les sait rafraîchir, en pleurant . . .

As well as Verlaine's rhythms, his rhymes are important too in this respect, for he makes no attempt to cultivate rich rhymes in the way that Baudelaire does, that is to say he does not try to find words with several elements rhyming, such as 'havane', 'savane', 'pavane' and 'caravane' in Baudelaire's 'Sed non satiata'; on the contrary he prefers to keep his rhymes as weak as possible as a further means of avoiding any oratorical note in, for example 'L'Heure du Berger':

> La lune est rouge au brumeux horizon;
> Dans un brouillard qui danse, la prairie
> S'endort fumeuse, et la grenouille crie
> Par les joncs verts où circule un frisson . . .

Not only do such poems herald what was to become Verlaine's distinctive versification, but as regards their imagery too they have an already characteristic Verlainian tone in their use of misty autumn landscapes at sunset or in the moonlight and it is by means of these blurred, 'tearful' images more than by means of any actual statements the poems make that they achieve their effect, which is emotional rather than intellectual. 'Chanson d'Automne' is a particularly good example of this aspect of Verlaine's technique in that there is no detailed definition or analysis of his feelings which are conveyed instead through the images of the sad note of violins in autumn, the sound of a clock striking and dead leaves being blown hither and thither by the wind:

> Les sanglots longs
> Des violons
>   De l'automne
> Blessent mon cœur
> D'une langueur
>   Monotone.
>
> Tout suffocant
> Et blême, quand
>   Sonne l'heure,
> Je me souviens
> Des jours anciens
>   Et je pleure;
>
> Et je m'en vais
> Au vent mauvais
>   Qui m'emporte
> Deçà, delà,
> Pareil à la
>   Feuille morte.

It is by the accumulation of such images in this and other poems, as well as by the fleeting, hesitant rhythms and the tenuous rhymes that Verlaine's poetry acquires that strange quality of indefinable sadness that was to become its particular hallmark. Despite the statement of his friend and biographer Edmond Lepelletier that 'dans ce recueil juvénile il n'y a aucune expression intime, aucun aveu, aucune trace de confession',[3] it is difficult to doubt that the sense of instability they convey, the sense of someone adrift who feels the desperate need for a firm anchorage, springs from the circumstances of Verlaine's life at that time. J. H. Bornecque in fact claims to identify, in his critical edition of *Poèmes saturniens*, certain specific experiences, and in particular he believes that one can detect, in the section entitled *Melancholia*, a cycle of sonnets inspired by Elisa Moncomble whom he sees as the mysterious and consoling figure in 'Mon Rêve familier', 'Vœu', 'A une Femme' and 'Nevermore' while a return visit to Elisa's home inspired, he contends, 'Après Trois Ans'.[4]

As a consequence of all these features, the indefinable sadness, the blurred imagery, the fluid and hesitant rhythms and the tenuous rhymes, much of the poetry of Verlaine's first volume of verse is, paradoxically, very far removed from the kind of poetry advocated in the 'Prologue' and the 'Epilogue' to the volume. Many of the poems have none of the clarity of line and colour implied by the analogy with sculpture; on the contrary they already herald the analogy between poetry and music which Verlaine, moving from the Parnassian to the Symbolist aesthetic, was to make a few years later in the opening line of his 'Art poétique': 'De la musique avant toute chose'. He himself recognised in fact, in the preface he added to the second edition of *Poèmes saturniens* in 1890, that his later, authentic manner could already be detected in his first volume of verse:

Il serait des plus facile à quelqu'un qui croirait que cela en valût la peine, de retracer les pentes d'habitude devenues le lit, profond ou non, clair ou bourbeux, où s'écoulent mon style et ma manière actuels, notamment l'un peu déjà libre versification, enjambements et rejets dépendant plus généralement des deux césures avoisinantes, fréquentes allitérations, quelque chose comme de l'assonance souvent dans le corps du vers, rimes plutôt rares que riches, le mot propre évité des fois à dessein ou presque. En même temps la pensée triste et voulue telle ou crue voulue telle.[5]

It is however surprising that Verlaine should have made this comment as late as 1890 and should have talked of 'mon style et ma manière *actuels*' when in fact, by that date, he was no longer writing the kind of poetry he defines so precisely. He had returned instead to a different kind of poetry that can also be detected here and there in *Poèmes saturniens*, a poetry with a curiously contrived look about it and which goes into far too much irrelevant detail, often, it seems, for the sole purpose of finding a more or less suitable rhyme at any cost:

> Puis je louerai beaucoup, comme il convient,
>   Cette chair bénie
> Dont le parfum opulent me revient
>   Les nuits d'insomnie . . .

The utter banality of these lines from 'Sérénade' is matched by the lines describing the portrait of César Borgia where Verlaine writes of

> . . . la pâleur mate et belle du visage
> Vu de trois quarts, et très ombré, suivant l'usage
> Des Espagnols, ainsi que des Vénitiens
> Dans les portraits de rois et de patriciens.

The presence of lines of this sort in *Poèmes saturniens* should not be ignored since they bear witness to the fact that Verlaine was capable, even at this early stage, of turning out verse that is very far removed indeed from his best poetry. Throughout his life, and increasingly in his later years, as will be seen, he was to publish the two kinds side by side, apparently unaware of the vast difference in quality between them.

Fêtes galantes

In Verlaine's second volume, published early in 1869, *Fêtes galantes*, his ostensible purpose was to transpose into verse the paintings of such eighteenth-century artists as Watteau, Fragonard, Lancret and Boucher who, towards the middle of the nineteenth century, had come back into fashion. In 1850 a volume of reproductions of engravings of Watteau's pictures had appeared and in 1854 a study entitled *Les Peintres des Fêtes galantes* had been published by the art historian Charles Blanc. It may well be that it was from this latter source that Verlaine borrowed his title, although two even more important works which turned his attention towards Watteau and his contemporaries were no doubt the essay on Watteau published by the Goncourt brothers in 1860, later to form part of their lengthy study *L'Art du XVIIIe siècle*, and, in the same year, the *Histoire de l'Art français au XVIIIe siècle* by Arsène Houssaye who was the editor of the magazine *L'Artiste* in which eight of the poems of *Fêtes galantes* were to appear in 1868 and 1869. Nor should the probable influence of one of the leading poets and art critics of the day be ignored, namely Théophile Gautier, whose affection for the eighteenth century was displayed in the series of enthusiastic articles he wrote in 1860 about an exhibition which included the

Watteau paintings in the extensive Lacaze collection later to be left to the Louvre.[6]

Not only did eighteenth-century painting thus come back into vogue but there was also a renewal of interest in Shakespearian comedy and in the Italian 'commedia dell' arte' which have something of the same fantasy quality as Watteau's paintings. It may therefore be that Verlaine drew upon these sources too when composing his *Fêtes galantes*.

He was, however, by no means the first poet of the period to be affected by this taste for costumed figures living in a world divorced from reality. On the contrary, he was, in this respect, the culmination of a poetic tradition going back some twenty or thirty years.[7] One of the early landmarks in the development of this kind of poetry was Gautier's 'Variations sur le Carnaval de Venise' in 1849 depicting Arlequin, Colombine, Polichinelle and Scaramouche (all of whom re-appear in Verlaine's *Fêtes galantes*) wending their way across Venice to a masked ball. Four years later, in 1853, Banville published a poem entitled 'Arlequin et Colombine' in which he placed these two figures in a setting of flowers and fountains peopled by nymphs and Cupids. In 1856 Hugo included in *Les Contemplations* a poem composed as early as 1840, 'La Fête chez Thérèse', in which guests wander through gardens dressed as characters from Italian comedy and in *Les Chansons des Rues et des Bois* in 1865 he published 'Lettre' depicting himself seeking refuge from a dissatisfying dream in the contemplation of a typical eighteenth-century painting of lovers in an idyllic landscape. Meanwhile, in 1857, Baudelaire had devoted one of the stanzas of 'Les Phares' in *Les Fleurs du Mal* to an evocation of the essential qualities of Watteau's art:

> Watteau, ce carnaval où bien des cœurs illustres,
> Comme des papillons, errent en flamboyant,
> Décors frais et légers éclairés par des lustres
> Qui versent la folie à ce bal tournoyant.

Finally, Verlaine himself, in one of the *Poèmes saturniens*, 'Nuit du Walpurgis classique', had already described a 'jardin de Lenôtre' and in this Watteau-like setting of avenues and fountains, clipped hedges and marble statues, he had placed

> . . . des formes toutes blanches,
> Diaphanes, et que le clair de lune fait
> Opalines parmi l'ombre verte des branches . . .

To some extent therefore Verlaine was simply following the current fashion in *Fêtes galantes* and trying to convey in poetry all the carefree gaiety of the Regency period in the early eighteenth century that Watteau had conveyed in his painting. The lovers in 'A la Promenade' are

> Trompeurs exquis et coquettes charmantes,
> Cœurs tendres mais affranchis de serments,

Faces are playfully slapped, hands are kissed with a mock boldness, ostensibly cold glances are belied by tender smiles:

> . . . les amants lutinent les amantes
>
> De qui la main imperceptible sait
> Parfois donner un soufflet qu'on échange
> Contre un baiser sur l'extrême phalange
> Du petit doigt, et comme la chose est
>
> Immensément excessive et farouche,
> On est puni par un regard très sec,
> Lequel contraste, au demeurant, avec
> La moue assez clémente de la bouche.

The skaters in 'En patinant' prefer

> Des baisers superficiels
> Et des sentiments à fleur d'âme.

In the spring their five senses are stimulated but

> . . . seuls, tout seuls, bien seuls et sans
> Que la crise monte à la tête,

and when, in the heat of summer, they succumb to 'un vent de lourde volupté' they later deplore their folly:

> Nous cédâmes à tout cela,
> Et ce fut un bien ridicule
> Vertigo qui nous affola
> Tant que dura la canicule.

They welcome the arrival of autumn:

• •

> L'automne, heureusement, avec
> Son jour froid et ses bises rudes,
> Vint nous corriger, bref et sec,
> De nos mauvaises habitudes,

and in winter they return to their life of untroubled pleasure. The 'exquise fièvre' experienced by the two lovers who figure in 'Cythère' is belied by the practical considerations of the last lines of the poem:

> Et l'Amour comblant tout, hormis
> La Faim, sorbets et confitures
> Nous préservent des courbatures.

In 'Lettre', on several occasions, a short, sharp phrase punctures the grandiose sentiments of the preceding lines, as at the very beginning of the poem:

> Eloigné de vos yeux, Madame, par des soins
> Impérieux (j'en prends tous les dieux à témoins)
> Je languis et me meurs, comme c'est ma coutume
> En pareil cas . . .

Elsewhere Verlaine evokes not only the careless gaiety but also the moral laxity of the Regency period, and the tone of such poems as 'En Bateau', 'Les Indolents', 'Les Ingénus', 'Cortège' and 'Les Coquillages' is, as one critic puts it, 'plus gaulois que galant'.[8] But this slightly bawdy or, to use a perhaps more appropriate term, slightly naughty interest in shapely ankles, bare shoulders and the suggestive shapes of sea-shells nevertheless has the same playful, superficial quality, on the sensual level, as the sentiments expressed by the lovers in *Fêtes galantes* have on the emotional level.

On occasions, however, these outwardly gay and carefree revellers are 'quasi tristes sous leurs déguisements fantasques' and an unexpected depth of feeling can suddenly occur in what have, until then, seemed light-hearted affairs. In 'Colombine' Verlaine asks, in the last two verses:

> Oh! dis-moi vers quels
> Mornes ou cruels
> Désastres

> L'implacable enfant
> Preste et relevant
>   Ses jupes,
> La rose au chapeau,
> Conduit son troupeau
>   De dupes?

and this same 'implacable enfant', in the last verse of another poem, 'Pantomime', discovers, to her astonishment, that genuine emotions have been stirred:

> Colombine rêve, surprise
> De sentir un cœur dans la brise
> Et d'entendre en son cœur des voix.

The tempting glimpses of 'bas de jambes' and 'nuques blanches' in 'Les Ingénus' lead into a final verse where deeper feelings are revealed:

> Le soir tombait, un soir équivoque d'automne:
> Les belles, se pendant rêveuses à nos bras,
> Dirent alors des mots si spécieux, tout bas,
> Que notre âme depuis ce temps tremble et s'étonne.

The lovers in 'Le Faune' are described as 'mélancoliques pèlerins' and at the end of 'Mandoline' a note of sadness creeps in with the mention of the 'frissons de brise'.

In thus seeing the hidden melancholy behind the outer mask of gaiety in eighteenth-century painting, Verlaine was not being startlingly original. The Goncourt brothers, referring to Watteau's figures, had written of 'la vague harmonie qui murmure derrière les paroles rieuses' and of 'la tristesse musicale et doucement contagieuse répandue dans ces fêtes galantes',[9] and Baudelaire's quatrain quoted above hints at the doom awaiting these revellers towards the end of the century. But does this mean that, as has sometimes been claimed, *Fêtes galantes* is purely and simply an evocation of the mood of the eighteenth century as expressed by its painters and that it is a completely impersonal volume with nothing in it of Verlaine's own feelings? It is perhaps significant that in 'Nuit du Walpurgis classique' Verlaine had asked:

> Ces spectres agités, sont-ce donc la pensée
> Du poète ivre, ou son regret, ou son remords . . .

and behind the eighteenth-century façade of costumed figures, half gay, half sad, in *Fêtes galantes* there seems to be good reason for perceiving the lonely, moody figure of the 'poète saturnien' himself, still in pursuit of his dream of 'une femme inconnue, et que j'aime, et qui m'aime'. It may well be in fact that Verlaine turned towards the eighteenth century not so much because of current fashion but because he saw in these figures in Watteau's paintings the image of his own instability. He too would, no doubt, have preferred 'des sentiments à fleur d'âme', but he too, no doubt, found that his emotions could be stirred far more deeply than he had intended:

> Calmes dans le demi-jour
> Que les branches hautes font,
> Pénétrons bien notre amour
> De ce silence profond.
>
> Fondons nos âmes, nos cœurs
> Et nos sens extasiés,
> Parmi les vagues langueurs
> Des pins et des arbousiers.

But he was clearly unsuccessful in achieving a stable relationship at this deeper level, judging by the following lines from 'L'Amour par terre' in which it is surely Verlaine himself who is speaking:

> . . . des pensers mélancoliques vont
> Et viennent dans mon rêve où le chagrin profond
> Evoque un avenir solitaire et fatal.

The lesson of the final poem of *Fêtes galantes*, 'Colloque sentimental', is of the ephemeral nature of love and of the impossibility of two people forging a lasting relationship, and again one feels that the two figures in the poem are not only ghosts from the past and from eighteenth-century history but also ghosts from the future and from Verlaine's own personal fears:

> Dans le vieux parc solitaire et glacé
> Deux formes ont tout à l'heure passé.
>
> Leurs yeux sont morts et leurs lèvres sont molles,
> Et l'on entend à peine leurs paroles.
>
> Dans le vieux parc solitaire et glacé
> Deux spectres ont évoqué le passé.

—Te souvient-il de notre extase ancienne?
—Pourquoi voulez-vous donc qu'il m'en souvienne?

Ton cœur bat-il toujours à mon seul nom?
Toujours vois-tu mon âme en rêve?—Non.

—Ah! les beaux jours de bonheur indicible
Où nous joignions nos bouches!—C'est possible.

—Qu'il était bleu, le ciel, et grand, l'espoir!
—L'espoir a fui, vaincu, vers le ciel noir.

Tels ils marchaient dans les avoines folles,
Et la nuit seule entendit leurs paroles.

Despite its eighteenth-century setting *Fêtes galantes* therefore continues the mood of sadness that had made its appearance in *Poèmes saturniens*, and it also continues the first volume as regards imagery and versification. Verlaine is more than ever the poet of twilight and moonlight—'Clair de Lune' is the title of the first poem in *Fêtes galantes* and the last poem, 'Colloque sentimental' ends with the words of the ghostly couple being lost in the night air; in between these opening and closing scenes most of the poems have as their background the 'ciel si pâle' of 'A la Promenade', or the 'soir équivoque d'automne' of 'Les Ingénus', or the 'faible odeur des roses' of 'Cythère', or the 'lune rose et grise' of 'Mandoline' or the 'demi-jour' created by the overhanging branches in 'En Sourdine'. In these settings Verlaine is more than ever a poet who feels most at ease with the short poem written in short lines with weak rhymes and a fluid rhythm so that a curiously fleeting quality is achieved. The long-winded Parnassian composer of rather self-conscious descriptive and narrative verse has almost completely disappeared and only two poems exceed twenty lines in length compared with about a dozen in the earlier volume. In *Poèmes saturniens* half the poems were in traditional alexandrines, whereas the proportion is reduced to about one-fifth in *Fêtes galantes* with not a single sonnet compared to the half dozen in the earlier volume. On the other hand, fourteen poems in *Fêtes galantes*, compared with only about half that number in *Poèmes saturniens*, are in lines of eight syllables or less. Two of these, 'Mandoline' and 'En Sourdine' are in 'vers impairs' of seven syllables and another one, 'Colombine', in an unusual combination of five-syllable and two-syllable lines, so that Verlaine maintains his liking for the uneven line. These two poems are also worthy of note in that 'En Sourdine', like 'Un Dahlia' and 'Croquis parisien' in *Poèmes saturniens*, is in exclusively masculine rhymes and 'Mandoline' in exclusively feminine rhymes. There is the same tendency as in *Poèmes saturniens* to make a generous use of 'enjambement' and in general to break down any regular rhythmic pattern, the most outstanding example being 'A Clymène' which, like 'Le Rossignol' and other poems in the earlier volume, is made up of a single flowing sentence:

> Mystiques barcarolles,
> Romances sans paroles,
> Chère, puisque tes yeux,
> Couleur des cieux,
>
> Puisque ta voix, étrange
> Vision qui dérange
> Et trouble l'horizon
> De ma raison
>
> Puisque l'arôme insigne
> De ta pâleur de cygne
> Et puisque la candeur
> De ton odeur,
>
> Ah! puisque tout ton être,
> Musique qui pénètre,
> Nimbes d'anges défunts,
> Tons et parfums,
>
> A, sur d'almes cadences,
> En ces correspondances
> Induit mon cœur subtil,
> Ainsi soit-il!

The same kind of irregular repetitions occur as in *Poèmes saturniens*, in, for example, 'Colloque sentimental' that has been quoted above, or towards the end of 'Clair de Lune'

> Et leur chanson se mêle au clair de lune,
>
> Au calme clair de lune triste et beau,
> Qui fait rêver les oiseaux dans les arbres
> Et sangloter d'extase les jets d'eau,
> Les grands jets d'eau sveltes parmi les marbres.

or in 'L'Amour par terre':

> Le vent de l'autre nuit a jeté bas l'Amour ...
>
> Le vent de l'autre nuit l'a jeté bas! Le marbre
> Au souffle du matin tournoie, épars. C'est triste
> De voir le piédestal, où le nom de l'artiste
> Se lit péniblement parmi l'ombre d'un arbre,
>
> Oh! c'est triste de voir debout le piédestal
> Tout seul! ...

In *Fêtes galantes* Verlaine is therefore clearly continuing to develop the technical freedom with which he had begun to experiment in *Poèmes saturniens*, as Arthur Rimbaud was to recognise in a letter to Georges Izambard on 25 August 1870 in which he drew attention to the total absence of a caesura in one of the infrequent alexandrines of *Fêtes galantes*: 'Parfois de fortes licences: ainsi "et la tigresse épou-vantable d'Hyrcanie" est un vers de ce volume.' Furthermore, there is scarcely a single poem, or even a single line, where Verlaine's poetic skill has deserted him and he is never forced into the flat, dull, prosaic kind of verse that can be perceived here and there in *Poèmes saturniens*. Few, if any, critics would in fact disagree with Rimbaud's perceptive judgement of the volume as a whole: 'C'est fort bizarre, très drôle; mais vraiment c'est adorable.'[10]

La Bonne Chanson

More than twelve months before this comment however, Verlaine had become engaged to Mathilde Mauté in the early summer of 1869, shortly after the appearance of *Fêtes galantes*, and the volume of verse that resulted from the engagement was *La Bonne Chanson*. Although it was not put on sale until 1872, because of the Franco-Prussian war and the troubles of the Commune, the volume was actually printed in June 1870 and was intended to coincide with the marriage, which was also originally fixed for that month, but was in fact put off until August in order to enable Mathilde to recover from an attack of chicken pox. It is to this illness that Verlaine refers in a poem dated 5 July 1870 which he added as a preface to later editions of *La Bonne Chanson* and which exemplifies all the faults of this third volume of verse where the authentic Verlainian note that had made its appearance in some of the *Poèmes saturniens* and had developed still further in *Fêtes galantes* suffers a severe setback. The indefinable sadness, the blurred imagery, the fluid rhythms, the hesitant note, all these features have disappeared from the opening poem of *La Bonne Chanson* with its cry of: 'Espérons, ma mie, espérons!', its description of the smiling future that awaits the happy couple:

> L'avenir, le front couronné
> De fleurs qu'un joyeux soleil dore,

and the faintly ludicrous gravity of the allusion to Mathilde's illness:

> Faut-il qu'au moment tant béni
> Ce mal affreux t'ait disputée
> A ma tendresse épouvantée
> Et de ton chevet m'ait banni?

This tendency to define, and even to over-define, which Verlaine had already displayed on occasions in *Poèmes saturniens* but which had disappeared from *Fêtes galantes*, is typical of the vast majority of the poems of *La Bonne Chanson*, some of which must surely have embarrassed even the naïve Mathilde herself by their excessively lavish and detailed compliments. The following verse from the second poem in the collection is a notable example of this kind of thing:

> L'intelligence vient chez elle
> En aide à l'âme noble; elle est
> Pure autant que spirituelle:
> Ce qu'elle a dit, il le fallait!

Even more deplorable is the third verse of the third poem:

> Sa voix, étant de la musique fine,
> Accompagnait délicieusement
> L'esprit sans fiel de son babil charmant
> Où la gaîté d'un cœur bon se devine.

Other poems consist not of a series of definitions of Mathilde's many and varied qualities, but of a series of promises by Verlaine to reform his own many and varied faults:

> Arrière aussi les poings crispés et la colère
> A propos des méchants et des sots rencontrés;
> Arrière la rancune abominable! arrière
> L'oubli qu'on cherche en des breuvages exécrés!

or of a series of firm resolutions for the future:

> N'est-ce pas? en dépit des sots et des méchants
> Qui ne manqueront pas d'envier notre joie,
> Nous serons fiers parfois et toujours indulgents.

Elsewhere he describes in no less laborious terms his present situation rather than his past misdeeds and his future hopes, as, for example, when he complains about the long period of separation from Mathilde that he had to suffer when she was away on holiday in the summer of 1869:

> Quinze longs jours encore et plus de six semaines
> Déjà! Certes, parmi les angoisses humaines,
> La plus dolente angoisse est celle d'être loin . . .

The sense of stability and sense of direction that Mathilde Mauté brought into Verlaine's life, though no doubt having an excellent influence on his character, clearly had a disastrous effect on his poetry. Now that he was able to see his goal clearly he was no longer trying to express a vague 'état d'âme' by means of a misty landscape, and it is indeed a significant feature of *La Bonne Chanson* that its poems should so often be bathed in sunshine. 'Soleil', 'scintille', 'éclat', 'candeur', 'aube', 'aurore', 'clarté', 'grand jour', 'jour d'été', 'ciel clair', 'azur'—this is the kind of vocabulary which dominates *La Bonne Chanson* and gives it a completely different tonality from *Poèmes saturniens* and *Fêtes galantes*.

Furthermore, not only has the vague melancholy of the earlier volumes been replaced by a note of joyful certainty, and the blurred imagery by sunlit scenes, but the versification too shows a marked retreat from the fluidity towards which Verlaine had been moving in *Poèmes saturniens* and *Fêtes galantes*. The number of poems in alexandrines has increased again to almost half the total, while the number of poems in lines of eight syllables or less has dropped from fourteen to ten out of the same figure of twenty-two poems in both *Fêtes galantes* and *La Bonne Chanson*. There is far less use of 'enjambement' so that most of the poems are quite lacking in that sinuous, flowing line which was so striking in the two earlier volumes. The hesitant note too has disappeared along with the irregular repetitions and the seemingly spontaneous addition of one word after another. Verlaine no longer dreams vaguely of

> . . . une femme inconnue, et que j'aime, et qui m'aime,
> Et qui n'est, chaque fois, ni tout à fait la même
> Ni tout à fait une autre, et m'aime et me comprend.

Instead he recalls in precise detail

> Le souvenir charmant de cette jeune fille,
> Blanche apparition qui chante et qui scintille.

There are however one or two exceptions to this general loss of quality in *La Bonne Chanson*, the most notable being the only poem which has a moonlight setting and is written in four-syllable lines—two outward indications that this is something much more in the true Verlainian manner:

> La lune blanche
> Luit dans les bois;
> De chaque branche
> Part une voix
> Sous la ramée . . .
>
> O bien-aimée.

Here there is no attempt at intellectual definition but simply an evocation of a landscape conveying the poet's deeply felt emotion. Only in the final line is there any suggestion that this is a love poem, in contrast with another poem, much more typical of *La Bonne Chanson*, which uses the same setting of birds singing as two lovers in a wood at night, but in a much more prosaic and obvious way:

> Isolés dans l'amour ainsi qu'en un bois noir
> Nos deux cœurs, exhalant leur tendresse paisible
> Seront deux rossignols qui chantent dans le soir.

The second verse of 'La lune blanche...' continues to depict a shadowy landscape and to convey through this means the mood of the poet, with again no more than a casual suggestion in the final line that two people are involved:

> L'étang reflète,
> Profond miroir,
> La silhouette
> Du saule noir
> Où le vent pleure . . .
>
> Rêvons, c'est l'heure.

After the moonlit woods of the first verse and the dark ponds of the second verse, the third and final verse completes the picture by describing a starlit sky and once more the profound happiness of the lovers is neither overtly stated nor painstakingly analysed but simply conveyed:

> Un vaste et tendre
> Apaisement
> Semble descendre
> Du firmament
> Que l'astre irise . . .
>
> C'est l'heure exquise.

Typically, as regards Verlaine's authentic manner, but exceptionally in *La Bonne Chanson*, there is no punctuation in this final stanza where one line flows into another, and this same fluid quality is almost as marked in the other stanzas. The versification too has an originality unusual in *La Bonne Chanson*, though characteristic of Verlaine's best poetry, in that there appear to be three five-line stanzas with a detached line after each stanza, although in fact, from the point of view of the rhyme scheme, the poem is made up of alternate quatrains and couplets. What Verlaine has done is to attach the first line of the couplet to the preceding quatrain, thus leaving the second line suspended in mid-air, so to speak, in a most effective fashion. It is worth noting too that all three couplets are in feminine rhymes and that the quatrains have alternately masculine and feminine rhymes so that, in the poem as a whole, there are twice as many feminine rhymes as masculine rhymes, thus giving the poem a soft and gentle note. This is still further enchanced by the assonance between the first and the second stanza, with 'miroir' and 'noir' echoing 'bois' and 'voix', and by the presence of the vowel sound '–en' in each of the first four rhymes of the final stanza, so that this deliberate sameness creates an impression of undisturbed peace and stillness.

There are some critics, such as Jacques Borel[11] who contend that this is the only poem of *La Bonne Chanson* where the real Verlaine can be seen, but others, such as Antoine Adam[12] and Eléonore Zimmermann[13] prefer to add the poem which immediately precedes it, 'Avant que tu ne t'en ailles . . .', written in an unusual combination of three seven-syllable lines and one three-syllable line in each stanza. It is true that there is a dawn setting in the poem, but it is that moment of half-light as the last star disappears just before the sun rises. Much of the fascination of the poem lies in the way Verlaine interweaves these separate strands, devoting the first two lines of each stanza to the dying of the night and the second two lines of each stanza to the dawning of the day, the change of rhythm in the third line sharply marking the change in subject matter and the break in syntax. Towards the end of the poem this transition from darkness to light is associated with the awakening from sleep of the girl to whom the poet is trying to convey his thoughts in her dreams before she fully returns to reality:

> Avant que tu ne t'en ailles,
> Pâle étoile du matin,
> —Mille cailles
> Chantent, chantent dans le thym.—
>
> Tourne devers le poète,
> Dont les yeux sont pleins d'amour,
>   —L'alouette
> Monte au ciel avec le jour.—
>
> Tourne ton regard que noie
> L'aurore dans son azur;
>   —Quelle joie
> Parmi les champs de blé mûr!—
>
> Puis fais luire ma pensée
> Là-bas, —bien loin, oh! bien loin,
>   —La rosée
> Gaîment brille sur le foin.—
>
> Dans le doux rêve où s'agite
> Ma mie endormie encor . . .
>   —Vite, vite,
> Car voici le soleil d'or!—

But it is what is implicit in the poem rather than what is explicit that is really important—the sense of overwhelming happiness that is conveyed by the description of the landscape in the last two lines in each stanza with the quails singing, the lark flying up into the sky, the joy of the birds among the ripe corn and the sparkle of the sun on the grass. Behind these symbols there lies an intense emotion, just as there does behind the symbols of the pale moon, the singing birds, the dark pond, the weeping willow and the starlit sky in 'La lune blanche...'. In these two poems therefore Verlaine is using imagery in a far more subtle way than in, for example, the fourth poem in *La Bonne Chanson*, 'Puisque l'aube grandit, puisque voici l'aurore...', where he indulges in the most banal of metaphors which he repeats later in the poem:

> Car je veux, maintenant qu'un Etre de lumière
> A dans ma nuit profonde émis cette clarté...

In 'Avant que tu ne t'en ailles...' and 'La lune blanche...' he does not so much *state* that Mathilde has brought into his life the radiance of sunshine, or the peace and tranquillity of a moonlit landscape; he actually *conveys* this feeling of radiance or tranquillity, making this the primary purpose of the poems with no more than a passing mention of the reason for his happiness.

III

THE MAJOR POETRY

Romances sans Paroles

Despite the promises of *La Bonne Chanson*, before Verlaine's marriage was much more than a year old he was to find himself once again in that state of uncertainty which seems to have been essential to the full flowering of his poetic genius. He was quite unable to resist the powerful influence exerted over him by Rimbaud after the latter's arrival in Paris in September 1871 and he gradually swung more and more away from his wife and more and more towards Rimbaud until he finally abandoned Mathilde altogether in the summer of 1872 and lived with Rimbaud, at first in Belgium, as the two poets spent a few weeks wandering through the country, and, as from September 1872, in London. Yet Verlaine was never able to dismiss Mathilde completely from his mind and to swing completely over to Rimbaud, so that, in many of the poems written during the period stretching from the autumn of 1871 to the spring of 1873 and published under the title *Romances sans Paroles* early in 1874, there is the same note of indecision as in the days before Mathilde had given him a temporary firmness of purpose.

This is particularly true of the first nine poems of *Romances sans Paroles*, collectively sub-titled *Ariettes oubliées*, so much so that it is on occasions difficult to decide whether certain poems are addressed to Mathilde or to Rimbaud. The very first poem is a case in point:

> C'est l'extase langoureuse,
> C'est la fatigue amoureuse,
> C'est tous les frissons des bois
> Parmi l'étreinte des brises,
> C'est, vers les ramures grises,
> Le chœur des petites voix . . .

Antoine Adam[1] assumes that it is Mathilde who is the subject of these lines which first appeared in the magazine *La Renaissance littéraire et artistique* on 18 May 1872. But one of the finest of

Rimbaud's *Illuminations*, 'Veillées I' uses the same kind of vocabulary and the same kind of syntax for a similar purpose in a similar setting:

> C'est le repos éclairé, ni fièvre ni langueur
>   sur le lit ou sur le pré.
> C'est l'ami ni ardent ni faible. L'ami.
> C'est l'aimée ni tourmentante ni tourmentée. L'aimée.
> L'air et le monde point cherchés. La vie.
> —Etait-ce donc ceci?
> —Et le rêve fraîchit.

It does therefore seem possible that Verlaine's poem may be about Rimbaud rather than Mathilde,[2] all the more so perhaps in view of the fact that the note of sadness creeping in towards the end of Rimbaud's poem also occurs in the last verse of 'C'est l'extase langoureuse . . .':

> Cette âme qui se lamente
> En cette plainte dormante
> C'est la nôtre, n'est-ce pas?
> La mienne, dis, et la tienne,
> Dont s'exhale l'humble antienne
> Par ce tiède soir tout bas.

The second of the *Ariettes* is much more clearly concerned with Verlaine's hesitation between Mathilde and Rimbaud and with his fear of ending up with neither companion. The poem was originally entitled 'Escarpolette' and this image of a swing, swaying now one way, now the other, occurs in the final lines:

> O mourir de cette mort seulette
> Que s'en vont, cher amour qui t'épeures,
> Balançant jeunes et vieilles heures!
> O mourir de cette escarpolette!

A similar kind of indecision is apparent in the celebrated third poem, 'Il pleure dans mon cœur . . .' where Verlaine acknowledges that his sadness is incapable of any clear and rational explanation:

> Il pleure sans raison
> Dans ce cœur qui s'écœure,
> Quoi! nulle trahison?
> Ce deuil est sans raison.

In view of the final lines of the poem where Verlaine admits that although he feels neither love nor hatred he is nevertheless sick at heart:

> C'est bien la pire peine
> De ne savoir pourquoi,
> Sans amour et sans haine,
> Mon cœur a tant de peine,

it seems likely that the poem is about Mathilde and his attempt to achieve a feeling of indifference towards her, but it is possible that it could be about Rimbaud and could have been written in December 1872 when Verlaine spent a solitary Christmas in London, Rimbaud having returned to Charleville. He may have been trying to reassure himself that Rimbaud's departure was of no particular significance in their relationship, and that, even if it was, he himself was not particularly disturbed by it.

The fourth poem 'Il faut, voyez-vous, nous pardonner les choses . . .' is usually thought to be about the Verlaine-Rimbaud relationship,[3] in view of the reference to the wish of the couple figuring in the poem to escape from the rest of mankind and to attain 'le frais oubli de ce qui nous exile'. But it is conceivable that, on the contrary, as Antoine Adam[4] and Jacques Borel[5] contend, the 'deux pleureuses' who are also, paradoxically, 'bien heureuses', may be Verlaine and Mathilde, although this suggestion ignores the curious resemblance between Verlaine's appeal in the poem: 'Soyons deux enfants . . .' and the words used by the 'vierge folle' in Rimbaud's *Une Saison en Enfer*: 'Je nous voyais comme deux bons enfants . . .' But whatever may be the identity of Verlaine's companion there is no doubt that he is torn between Mathilde and Rimbaud and that it is the conflict of these 'vœux confus' which constitutes the essential theme of the poem. The same may be said to be true of the fifth *Ariette*, 'Le piano que baise une main frêle . . .', in that this recollection by Verlaine of a moment in his life with Mathilde is coloured by the fact that it is a memory of something which no longer exists and for the loss of which he feels a profound regret. Behind a poem which at first glance seems to be concerned solely with Mathilde, the shadow of Rimbaud can therefore be perceived, especially in the seventh and eighth lines where Verlaine alludes to his present unhappiness and looks back longingly towards the comfort and shelter he had once enjoyed:

> Qu'est-ce c'est que ce berceau soudain
> Qui lentement dorlote mon pauvre être?

In the seventh *Ariette* on the other hand, 'O triste, triste était mon âme!...', it is the shadow of Mathilde which haunts Verlaine in his life with Rimbaud, described in conflicting terms as 'ce fier exil, ce triste exil'. Although he tries to convince himself that he has cut himself off heart and soul from Mathilde he still feels a sense of inconsolable loss:

> Bien que mon cœur, bien que mon âme
> Eussent fui loin de cette femme.
>
> Je ne me suis pas consolé
> Bien que mon cœur s'en soit allé ...

The eighth poem differs from the others in that, with the exception of the sixth, 'C'est le chien de Jean de Nivelle...,' which is little more than a prosodic 'tour de force' juggling with masculine and feminine rhymes, the preceding *Ariettes* express Verlaine's own personal emotions directly, with constant references to 'mon âme', 'mon cœur', 'âmes sœurs que nous sommes', 'cette âme ... c'est la nôtre', 'mon pauvre être', whereas 'Dans l'interminable Ennui de la plaine' expresses his emotions indirectly without any personal intervention by the poet. His 'état d'âme' is merely implied in the description of the sombre sky, the grey mist, the cold wind and the patches of snow, whereas those of the other *ariettes* which make use of symbolic scenes make an explicit comparison between them and the poet's mood. The most obvious example is the third *ariette*:

> Il pleure dans mon cœur
> Comme il pleut sur la ville,

but in the first one too, after a description of a woodland scene full of a 'frêle et frais murmure', Verlaine asks:

> Cette âme qui se lamente
> En cette plainte dormante
> C'est la nôtre, n'est-ce pas?

and in the fifth *ariette* as well, the second verse deals with the effect on the poet of the scene described in the first verse. Although some of the *Ariettes oubliées* such as the fourth and the seventh do not make use of symbolic scenes in this way, most of them do so and the ninth and last in fact acknowledges the extent to which Verlaine uses landscapes to express a mood:

> Combien, ô voyageur, ce paysage blême
> Te mira blême toi-même.

These two lines, from a poem dated 'mai-juin 1872', not only refer back to the *Ariettes oubliées* all of which were probably written before that date, they also serve as an introduction to the next section of *Romances sans Paroles* entitled *Paysages belges*, written in the summer of 1872 when Verlaine and Rimbaud were roaming across southern Belgium. The mood of these poems however is, on the whole, less sad than that of the *Ariettes oubliées*, possibly because once Verlaine had made the decision to leave Mathilde his feeling of anguish at being torn between her and Rimbaud was less acute. The first of the *Paysages belges* is in fact gay and carefree in its description of Walcourt:

> Briques et tuiles,
> O les charmants
> Petits asiles
> Pour les amants!

but it is surely a mistake to regard the poem, as Antoine Adam does,[6] as purely descriptive; the 'amants' of the first verse, like the 'francs buveurs' of the second, the 'fumeurs' of the third and the 'bons juifs errants' of the last verse are clearly Verlaine and Rimbaud so that the poem is much more personal than M. Adam seems to suppose. In other words this is once again a landscape reflecting the mood of the poet, only this time and most unusually, the mood is one of untroubled gaiety. In the second of the *Paysages belges*, 'Charleroi', the mood changes and is much nearer that of the *Ariettes oubliées*, due to such lines as:

> Le vent profond
> Pleure, on veut croire,

but the poem nevertheless has a sense of vigour and movement which is lacking in the *Ariettes oubliées* and which no doubt reflects the wandering life the two poets were leading at this period. The first of the two 'simples fresques' inspired by Brussels has an even greater feeling of sadness about it and with such lines as:

> Toutes mes langueurs rêvassent
> Que berce l'air monotone,

it would scarcely be out of place among the *Ariettes oubliées*, but the second one has, if not quite the gaiety of 'Walcourt', at least a certain tranquillity in the remark addressed to Rimbaud:

> Sais-tu qu'on serait
> Bien sous le secret
> De ces arbres-ci,

and in the wish expressed at the end of the poem:

> Le château, tout blanc,
> Avec, à son flanc,
> Le soleil couché,
> Les champs à l'entour ...
> Oh! que notre amour
> N'est-il là niché!

The same is true of the poem inspired by a fairground scene in Brussels, 'Tournez, tournez, bons chevaux de bois ...' where only in the last two verses does the jovial tone alter as Verlaine imagines 'le gros soldat, la plus grosse bonne' on their wooden horses being transported into a different world:

> Et dépêchez, chevaux de leur âme:
> Déjà, voici que la nuit qui tombe
> Va réunir pigeon et colombe,
> Loin de la foire et loin de madame.
>
> Tournez, tournez! le ciel en velours
> D'astres en or se vêt lentement.
> Voici partir l'amante et l'amant.
> Tournez au son joyeux des tambours.

As for the last of the *Paysages belges*, 'Malines', this does appear to be a purely descriptive poem, totally lacking in any attempt to evoke a mood, and in its solemn and even pompous account of the view from a train window it is reminiscent of some of the more laborious verses of *La Bonne Chanson*:

Les wagons filent en silence
Parmi ces sites apaisés.
Dormez, les vaches! Reposez,
Doux taureaux de la plaine immense,
Sous vos cieux à peine irisés!...[7]

The same judgement must be made of the third section of *Romances sans Paroles*, whose title, for no apparent reason, is taken from that of a cradle song by Sir Arthur Sullivan, 'Birds in the Night'. Although one critic has described this long poem, arranged in seven sections, each of three quatrains, as 'un des plus beaux et des plus déchirants poèmes que Verlaine ait écrits'[8] another critic holds a very different opinion: 'Le goût de l'anecdote sentimentale, du fait divers personnel, est trop ancré dans sa nature pour ne pas faire intrusion jusque dans les *Romances sans Paroles*. L'inspiration de *La Bonne Chanson* reparaît dans "Birds in the Night" '.[9] It is difficult to disagree with this judgement since even the most superficial reading of the poem reveals the same deplorable tendency towards over-definition that has been noted in many of the poems of *La Bonne Chanson*. It is no doubt significant that the first title that Verlaine thought of for the poem was 'La Mauvaise Chanson', since it is in fact a kind of companion piece to the earlier volume, the 'revers de la médaille' as Verlaine looks back at his marriage from a different viewpoint though still using the same analytical, descriptive approach with a wealth of laborious detail, lapsing, on more than one occasion, into painful banality:

Oui, je souffrirai, car je vous aimais!
Mais je souffrirai comme un bon soldat
Blessé, qui s'en va dormir à jamais,
Plein d'amour pour quelque pays ingrat.

Vous qui fûtes ma Belle, ma Chérie,
Encore que de vous vienne ma souffrance,
N'êtes-vous donc pas toujours ma Patrie,
Aussi jeune, aussi folle que la France?

As well as condemning the extreme platitude of such lines many critics find it intolerable that in 'Birds in the Night' Verlaine should have the impertinence to complain, apparently in contradiction to the facts of the situation, that it is he who has been abandoned by his wife:

> Vous n'avez pas eu toute patience,
> Cela se comprend par malheur, de reste;
> Vous êtes si jeune! et l'insouciance,
> C'est le lot amer de l'âge céleste! . . .
>
> Aussi, me voici plein de pardons chastes,
> Non, certes! joyeux, mais très calme, en somme,
> Bien que je déplore, en ces mois néfastes,
> D'être, grâce à vous, le moins heureux homme . . .

This view however fails to take account of the meaning of the enigmatic final section of the poem:

> Par instants je suis le pauvre navire
> Qui court démâté parmi la tempête.
> Et ne voyant pas Notre-Dame luire
> Pour l'engouffrement en priant s'apprête.
>
> Par instants je meurs la mort du pécheur
> Qui se sait damné s'il n'est confessé,
> Et, perdant l'espoir de nul confesseur,
> Se tord dans l'Enfer qu'il a devancé.
>
> O mais! par instants, j'ai l'extase rouge
> Du premier chrétien, sous la dent rapace,
> Qui rit à Jésus témoin, sans que bouge
> Un poil de sa chair, un nerf de sa face!

There is little doubt that the 'Jésus' of the final verse is Rimbaud and that the ardent 'premier chrétien' is Verlaine, whose sonnet 'Le Bon Disciple', which also uses Biblical names with the same métaphorical significance, was composed shortly before 'Birds in the Night'.[10] Verlaine is therefore emphasising that he is convinced, or is trying to convince himself, that he and Rimbaud are fulfilling some kind of spiritual mission and that, although he has his moments of doubt as to whether they will achieve their goal, and indeed moments of utter despair when he feels he has been led along quite the wrong path by Rimbaud, at other moments he is carried away by his conviction that Rimbaud does possess divine powers. If Verlaine firmly believed that this was so (and the sub-chapter of Rimbaud's *Une Saison en Enfer* entitled *Délires I*, 'Vierge folle, l'Époux infernal' supports this view, as does Verlaine's 'Crimen Amoris' in *Jadis et Naguère*) then it seems less unreasonable that he should have been prepared to abandon his wife and family in order to follow 'celui-là qui sera Dieu' to quote from the first version of 'Crimen Amoris'. But although this explanation makes such lines as: 'Vous n'avez pas eu toute patience', and: 'Aussi, me voici plein de pardons chastes', appear rather more acceptable, it does not alter the fact that the poem as a whole is singularly lacking in that capacity to create an 'état d'âme' which characterises most of the *Ariettes oubliées* and the *Paysages belges*.

The fourth section of *Romances sans Paroles*, entitled *Aquarelles*, contains two poems which are clearly extensions of 'Birds in the Night'. Were it not for the fact that it is in alexandrines instead of ten-syllable lines, 'Green' would seem like a detached section of the longer poem since it too is made up of three quatrains and is another plea for sympathy and understanding addressed to Mathilde with again, in the paradoxical expression: 'la bonne tempête', the refusal to admit, at this stage, that the adventure with Rimbaud is a failure.

> Sur votre jeune sein laissez rouler ma tête
> Toute sonore encor de vos derniers baisers;
> Laissez-la s'apaiser de la bonne tempête,
> Et que je dorme un peu puisque vous reposez.

As for 'Child Wife', the title of which was borrowed from Dickens' *David Copperfield*, the theme is again Mathilde's lack of understanding with again an accumulation of sometimes ludicrous details that make this probably the worst poem in *Romances sans Paroles* and one which in places plumbs depths unequalled even in *La Bonne Chanson*:

> Et vous gesticulez avec vos petits bras
>   Comme un héros méchant,
> En poussant d'aigres cris poitrinaires, hélas!
>   Vous qui n'étiez que chant!
>
> Car vous avez eu peur de l'orage et du cœur
>   Qui grondait et sifflait,
> Et vous bêlâtes vers votres mère—ô douleur!—
>   Comme un triste agnelet . . .

Of the five remaining poems in *Aquarelles*, *Spleen* is the most Verlainian in that it has a quality of mystery about it springing from the fact that the couplets, which are really divided quatrains, do not follow on logically one from another. It is as if two themes are pursued in parallel, rather as they were in 'Avant que tu ne t'en ailles . . .' in *La Bonne Chanson*, with, on the one hand, a description of a landscape in the first, the third and the fifth couplets and, on the other hand, an appeal to an unidentified companion in the second and fourth couplets with the two themes joining together in the final couplet:

> Les roses étaient toutes rouges,
> Et les lierres étaient tout noirs.
>
> Chère, pour peu que tu te bouges,
> Renaissent tous mes désespoirs.
>
> Le ciel était trop bleu, trop tendre,
> La mer trop verte et l'air trop doux.
>
> Je crains toujours, —ce qu'est d'attendre!—
> Quelque fuite atroce de vous.
>
> Du houx à la feuille vernie
> Et du luisant buis je suis las.
>
> Et de la campagne infinie,
> Et de tout, fors de vous, hélas!

Though there is nothing like the same air of mystery about 'Streets I', there is nevertheless a haunting quality about the gradual transition in the course of the poem from joy to sadness. The first two tercets are in the same vein as *La Bonne Chanson* with Verlaine offering clear and precise memories of the days when he and Mathilde were together:

> J'aimais surtout ses jolis yeux,
> Plus clairs que l'étoile des cieux,
> J'aimais ses yeux malicieux . . .
>
> Elle avait des façons vraiment
> De désoler un pauvre amant,
> Que c'en était vraiment charmant! . . .

But this clarity of detail gives way, after the sharp break in the third verse, to more vague and imprecise memories in the final verse which is reminiscent of the *Ariettes oubliées*:

> Mais je trouve encore meilleur
> Le baiser de sa bouche en fleur,
> Depuis qu'elle est morte à mon cœur . . .

Je me souviens, je me souviens
Des heures et des entretiens,
Et c'est le meilleur de mes biens . . .

and this increasingly sombre tone to the poem casts its shadow over the refrain: 'Dansons la gigue!' which, in the course of its five repetitions, acquires a melancholy note.

'Streets II', which could well have been entitled 'Paysage anglais' or more specifically 'Paysage londonien' since it depicts part of Regent's Canal,[11] is reminiscent of 'Malines' in *Paysages belges* in that it is no more than a simple description, going into too many concrete details to be poetically effective:

O la rivière dans la rue!
Fantastiquement apparue
Derrière un mur haut de cinq pieds,
Elle roule sans un murmure
Son onde opaque et pourtant pure,
Par les faubourgs pacifiés . . .

As for the last two poems in *Romances sans Paroles*, 'A Poor Young Shepherd' is a rather coy little love poem addressed to a mysterious Kate and may well be, as the title suggests, an attempt to create a kind of folk song, and 'Beams', written on board the cross Channel steamer taking Verlaine and Rimbaud from Dover to Ostend on 4 April 1873 is an account of the attention of the passengers being attracted by a mysterious and unidentified 'elle' who may well be the 'Comtesse de Flandre' specifically named at the end of the poem as the boat on which they were travelling.[12]

Not only is *Romances sans Paroles* thus a rather more uneven volume than is sometimes thought, ranging from the profound sadness of 'O triste, triste était mon âme . . .' to the querulous complaints of 'Child Wife' and from the evocative landscape of 'Dans l'interminable / Ennui de la plaine . . .' to the minutely detailed description of 'Malines', but there is a similar variation in the style of the poems. The *Ariettes oubliées* in particular have the same casual, quasi-spontaneous manner that has been noted in Verlaine's earlier volumes. The beginning of the last verse of the first of the *Ariettes* is a good example of this:

Cette âme qui se lamente
En cette plainte dormante

> C'est la nôtre, n'est-ce pas?
> La mienne, dis, et la tienne ...

and the same kind of conversational tone occurs in the opening of the fourth *Ariette*:

> Il faut, voyez-vous, nous pardonner les choses.
> De cette façon nous serons bien heureuses,
> Et si notre vie a des instants moroses,
> Du moins nous serons, n'est-ce pas? deux pleureuses.

Verlaine also makes use in the *Ariettes* of the linear construction, with its hesitations and repetitions and additions, that had been a feature of the best poems of *Poèmes saturniens* and *Fêtes galantes*. The most striking example of this technique is the seventh of the *Ariettes* where one has very much the impression that the poet is thinking aloud:

> O triste, triste était mon âme
> A cause, à cause d'une femme.
>
> Je ne me suis pas consolé
> Bien que mon cœur s'en soit allé,
>
> Bien que mon cœur, bien que mon âme
> Eussent fui loin de cette femme.
>
> Je ne me suis pas consolé,
> Bien que mon cœur s'en soit allé.
>
> Et mon cœur, mon cœur trop sensible
> Dit à mon âme: Est-il possible,
>
> Est-il possible, —le fût-il,—
> Ce fier exil, ce triste exil ...

The third poem too, 'Il pleure dans mon cœur . . .', with its constant repetition of the word 'cœur' which is to be found in each of the four verses though always in a different place, and is echoed in the verb 's'écœure' as well as in the verb 'pleure' twice repeated, is strongly reminiscent of the technique of 'Mon Rêve familier' and 'Soleils couchants' in *Poèmes saturniens* and 'L'Amour par terre' in *Fêtes galantes*.

The poems in the other sections of *Romances sans Paroles* however are, on the whole, lacking in this hesitant, repetitive quality. It is true that 'Walcourt' and 'Charleroi' have a certain informality about them, but this springs, not from a slow, reflective approach as in 'O triste, triste était mon âme . . .' but from the fact that they consist of a rapid succession of brief notations jotted down often with no verb—the shorter of the two poems, 'Walcourt', has in fact not a single verb throughout. On the other hand such poems as 'Birds in the Night', 'Green', 'Child Wife' and 'Beams' have a decidedly formal and composed character, with a logical train of thought expressed through a relatively complex sentence structure:

> Le soleil luisait haut dans le ciel calme et lisse,
> Et dans ses cheveux blonds c'étaient des rayons d'or,
> Si bien que nous suivions son pas plus calme encor
> Que le déroulement des vagues, ô délice!

There is a similar difference between the blurred settings of most of the *Ariettes oubliées*—the 'tiède soir' of the first poem, the 'jour trouble' of the second, the 'bruit doux de la pluie' in the third, the 'soir rose et gris vaguement' in the fifth, the 'ciel de cuivre' in the eighth, the 'rivière embrumée' in the ninth—and the much clearer, sharper images that occur elsewhere—the 'guinguettes claires' of 'Walcourt', the 'prés clairs' of 'Malines', the 'robe d'été blanche et jaune' of 'Birds in the Night', the 'vent du matin' of 'Green', the 'rayons d'or' of 'Beams'. It is true that 'Tournez, tournez, bons chevaux de bois . . .' refers, towards the end, to 'la nuit qui tombe' and that the second of the *Paysages belges*, 'Charleroi', has a darker tone which contrasts with its companion piece, 'Walcourt', while the third which, as has been said earlier, would scarcely be out of place in the *Ariettes oubliées*, depicts a landscape of muted colours and blurred outlines:

> La fuite est verdâtre et rose
> Des collines et des rampes,
> Dans un demi-jour de lampes
> Qui vient brouiller toute chose . . .

but on the whole the later sections of *Romances sans Paroles* are lacking in the twilight atmosphere that pervades the first section, just as they are, on the whole, lacking in the quasi-spontaneous, hesitant style of the *Ariettes oubliées*.

In the matter of versification however, *Romances sans Paroles* maintains almost throughout an extraordinary originality and variety. As Pierre Martino points out,[13] no two poems in the volume have the same form and Verlaine uses the whole range of possibilities—four-, five-, six-, seven-, eight-, nine-, ten-, eleven-, and twelve-syllable lines, grouped in verses of two, three, four, five and six lines. It is in the *Ariettes oubliées* that Verlaine is at his most original and of the nine poems in this section, four are in 'vers impairs', the first two in lines of seven and nine syllables respectively, the fourth in eleven-syllable lines and the eighth in five-syllable lines, while the ninth is partly in 'vers impairs' of seven syllables which alternate with alexandrines. Of the remaining four poems in 'vers pairs' the third is in six-syllable lines, the fifth in decasyllabic lines and the sixth and seventh in octosyllabic lines. Verlaine is therefore showing to an increasing degree that liking for the rapid rhythms of the shorter line and for the hesitancy of the 'vers impair' that he had already revealed in *Poèmes saturniens* and *Fêtes galantes*.

He also displays an increasing tendency to use unusual rhyme schemes. Four of the nine *Ariettes oubliées* are in exclusively feminine rhymes, namely 'Je devine à travers un murmure . . .', 'Il faut, voyez-vous, nous pardonner les choses . . .', 'Dans l'interminable/Ennui de la plaine . . .' and 'L'ombre des arbres dans la rivière embrumée . . .', while 'C'est le chien de Jean de Nivelle . . .' is even further removed from conventional practice in its use of false rhymes, that is rhymes which are phonetically correct but which are visually incorrect in that they bring together a masculine and a feminine rhyme:

> C'est le chien de Jean de Nivelle
> Qui mord, sous l'œil même du guet,
> Le chat de la mère Michel;
> François-les-bas-bleus s'en égaie.

This is no more than a defiant gesture of independence on Verlaine's part, but in the four poems in exclusively feminine rhymes his originality has another purpose in that it undoubtedly adds to the soft, indecisive note of these poems, as it had done to 'Mandoline' in *Fêtes galantes*. It is worth adding that in the case of another poem, 'C'est l'extase langoureuse . . .', Verlaine so arranges his lines, with each six-line stanza made up of a feminine couplet and a quatrain with two masculine and two feminine rhymes, as in 'La lune blanche . . .' in *La Bonne Chanson*, that there are twice as many feminine rhymes as masculine rhymes. The softening effect achieved by this preponderance of the mute 'e' sound is achieved in a quite different way in 'O triste, triste était mon âme . . .' where all the masculine rhymes without exception include the liquid consonant 'l' with its markedly attenuating effect. Verlaine's technical virtuosity in the *Ariettes*, however, reaches its height in the third poem where the second line of each of the four quatrains is left without any rhyme, but because of the extensive use of internal rhymes and a considerable amount of assonance and alliteration the presence of these 'rimes sans écho' passes unnoticed:

Il pleure dans mon cœur
Comme il pleut sur la ville.
Quelle est cette langueur
Qui pénètre mon cœur?

Il pleure sans raison
Dans ce cœur qui s'écœure.
Quoi! nulle trahison?
Ce deuil est sans raison.

O bruit doux de la pluie
Par terre et sur les toits!
Pour un cœur qui s'ennuie,
O le chant de la pluie!

C'est bien la pire peine
De ne savoir pourquoi,
Sans amour et sans haine
Mon cœur a tant de peine.

The rhyme for 'ville' in line 2 has really occurred in advance with the two pronouns 'il', at the beginning of line 1 and early in line 2, while the echo between 'pleure' and 'cœur' in line 1 allows one to accept the rhyme between 'langueur' and 'cœur' in lines 3 and 4 instead of a rhyme for 'ville'. Similarly in the second stanza, 'bruit' and 'pluie' in line 1 provide a pattern for the rhymes 'ennuie' and 'pluie' in lines 3 and 4 so that 'toits', helped by its alliteration with 'terre', can be accepted without a rhyme. The third stanza returns to the pattern of the first in that, like 'il', 'il' and 'ville', the words 'pleure' and 'cœur' provide a kind of advance rhyme for 's'écœure' which can therefore be left without any actual following rhyme, although the echo of this vowel in the word 'deuil' at the beginning of the fourth line further helps the absence of a true rhyme for 's'écœure' to pass unperceived. Finally the fourth stanza returns to the pattern of the second in the use of alliteration in 'pire peine' and internal rhyme in 'savoir pourquoi', so that the latter word, which also rhymes with 'toits' in the second stanza, can safely be left without a rhyme in the final line.

The six *Paysages belges* are only slightly less varied and enter-prising in their versification than the *Ariettes oubliées*. The two 'simples fresques' of Brussels are both in 'vers impairs', of seven syllables in one case and five in the other, the first being in ex-clusively feminine rhymes, thus adding to the effect of the muted colours and blurred outlines, and the second in exclusively masculine rhymes as befits a poem altogether lighter in tone than its companion piece. The third poem inspired by Brussels, 'Tournez, tournez, bons chevaux de bois . . .' is also in 'vers im-pairs', this time of nine syllables, with the verses being alter-nately in two masculine and two feminine rhymes. Of the remaining three poems in 'vers impairs' 'Walcourt' and 'Charleroi' help to convey the impression of people on the move by the use of the rapid rhythm of the short four-syllable line, while 'Malines' is in octosyllabic lines.

'Birds in the Night' is more conventional in its versification, although it is true that its ten-syllable lines are each divided into two groups of five syllables rather than into the more usual six-and four-syllable groups, and its verses, like those of 'Tournez, tournez, bons chevaux de bois . . .' are made up alternately of entirely feminine and entirely masculine rhymes.

As for the final section *Aquarelles* it too has its share of Verlainian versification, in that 'A Poor Young Shepherd' is in 'vers impairs' of five syllables and 'Child Wife' in exclusively masculine rhymes, as is 'Streets I' with the exception of the unrhymed refrain 'Dansons la gigue'. 'Streets II', however, and 'Spleen' are conventional in their rhyme schemes, as are 'Green' and 'Beams' which have a further air of conventionality by their use of alexandrines.

Viewed as a whole therefore, *Romances sans Paroles* is in no way fundamentally different from the works which precede it. It marks a resumption of Verlaine's progress, to a great extent interrupted by *La Bonne Chanson*, towards a distinctively personal style. There are still traces of a descriptive, analytical kind of verse, lapsing at times into utter banality, especially among those poems addressed reproachfully to Mathilde, but the majority of the poems, especially those in the first section, *Ariettes oubliées*, have the same indefinable sadness, the same blurred imagery, the same hesitant rhythm as the *Paysages tristes*, in particular, in

Poèmes saturniens, most of the *Fêtes galantes* and one or two poems of *La Bonne Chanson*. The very title *Romances sans Paroles*, borrowed from Mendelssohn's *Songs without Words*, implies that it is not the meaning of the poems that matters but their suggestive, musical quality. A similar idea of haunting but scarcely remembered melodies is implicit in the sub-title of the first section, *Ariettes oubliées*, and to some extent too in the sub-title of the last section *Aquarelles*, in that water-colours have that softness of outline that Verlaine sought to achieve. It should be added that one of the conclusions that must inevitably be drawn from this continuity of style between Verlaine's first four volumes of poetry is that, although Rimbaud had such a tremendous impact on Verlaine's life, his impact on his poetry was negligible. There is nothing in the style and technique of *Romances sans Paroles*, after Verlaine had met Rimbaud, that was not already present, even if to a lesser degree, in the style and technique of *Poèmes saturniens*, *Fêtes galantes* and *La Bonne Chanson*. The most that can be said is that there is rather more of the Verlainian kind of poetry in *Romances sans Paroles* than in the earlier volumes and that Rimbaud may therefore have encouraged Verlaine to develop his own personal manner to a greater degree than he might otherwise have done.[14]

Sagesse

Despite their similarities of style, Verlaine's volumes of poetry have so far been fairly clearly distinguished from one another by their subject matter. But no such clear line of demarcation can be drawn between *Romances sans Paroles* and Verlaine's next volume, *Sagesse*, published early in 1881. On the contrary, one of the descriptive poems of *Romances sans Paroles*, 'Tournez, tournez, bons chevaux de bois . . .' was also included in *Sagesse*, and two other poems in the latter volume, 'Le son du cor . . .' and 'La bise se rue . . .', written in all probability as early as April-May 1873 when Verlaine spent six weeks at Jehonville, could well have been included instead in *Romances sans Paroles*. They are in fact landscapes, closely related to 'Dans l'interminable / Ennui de la plaine . . .', not only by their probable date[15] and by their references to 'la neige qui tombe à longs traits de charpie / A

travers le coucher sanguinolent' and 'la neige éparpillée / Dans
la campagne ensoleillée', but also by their attempt to convey
through these landscapes an 'état d'âme'. 'Le son du cor . . .'
does indeed evoke a mood of sadness very similar to that of 'Dans
l'interminable / Ennui de la plaine . . .', although a gayer note is
struck in 'La bise se rue . . .',[16] not unlike that of 'Walcourt' in
Romances sans Paroles, and no doubt for similar reasons in that
Verlaine was looking forward to setting off to London once more
with Rimbaud.

Not only could these two landscapes in *Sagesse* equally well
have found a place in *Romances sans Paroles*, but the same is true
of a seascape, 'Je ne sais pourquoi . . .', originally entitled 'Sur
les eaux', which was almost certainly written on 3 July 1873
when Verlaine crossed the Channel alone after quarrelling with
Rimbaud in London. It might in fact have made a more suitable
ending for *Romances sans Paroles* than 'Beams' in that the latter is
bathed in an atmosphere of peace and tranquillity, whereas 'Je
ne sais pourquoi . . .' is much more typical of Verlaine's unhappiness at this period. As the opening line indicates, it has that
anxious, questioning note so often encountered in *Romances sans
Paroles*, and the first three lines:

> Je ne sais pourquoi
> Mon esprit amer
> D'une aile inquiète et folle vole sur la mer,

are like an echo of the last four lines of the third of the *Ariettes
oubliées*:

> C'est bien la pire peine
> De ne savoir pourquoi,
> Sans amour et sans haine,
> Mon cœur a tant de peine.

In order to fix the frontier between *Romances sans Paroles* and
Sagesse Verlaine seems therefore to have drawn a line at April
1873 which corresponds to no particular break in his life or in his
thoughts and feelings. At the time, however, when he and
Rimbaud had left London and crossed the Channel together on
4 April 1873 and had then gone their separate ways, Rimbaud to
Roche to begin *Une Saison en Enfer* and Verlaine to his relatives
at Jehonville, he may well have thought that a chapter in his life

was finished and that a new one was about to begin. By the time he realised that this was not so, when he met Rimbaud again on 24 May at Bouillon and set off with him once more for London, he had completed the manuscript of *Romances sans Paroles* and sent it to his friend Lepelletier in Paris for him to find a publisher.[17] Furthermore, although the date of July 1873, when the final quarrel with Rimbaud occurred, may now appear to mark a far more distinct break in Verlaine's life than the earlier date of April 1873, it is a break which is more apparent than real in the sense that, far from putting an end to his anxiety and uncertainty, his arrest merely replaced one form of stress and conflict with another. He now faced the prospect of being deprived of his liberty and a number of poems he wrote at this time, such as 'Le ciel est, par-dessus le toit', 'Un grand sommeil noir . . .' and 'L'espoir luit . . .' are concerned with this new dilemma in which he found himself, longing to return to the world outside the prison walls and yet fearing that he will have a lengthy sentence to serve.

This particular dilemma was resolved by his condemnation to two years imprisonment on 8 August 1873 and the confirmation of his sentence three weeks later on 27 August, but he still had one more profound emotional crisis to go through in the summer of 1874, namely his 'conversion', or, strictly speaking, his return to the Catholic faith in which he had been brought up. This meant yet another period of stress and conflict with Verlaine timidly aspiring towards God and yet fearing that he is unworthy of being welcomed into the fold. 'Du fond du grabat . . .' and more especially the celebrated dialogue between Verlaine and his Saviour beginning 'Mon Dieu m'a dit . . .' which forms the centre-piece of *Sagesse* are the two poems that give expression to this new crisis in Verlaine's life.

The completion of his return to Catholicism, however, meant that, as at the time of his engagement to Mathilde, he was lifted out of a state of instability and uncertainty into one of security and confidence which enabled him to view his new situation calmly and dispassionately. In consequence, like most of the poems of *La Bonne Chanson*, most of the later poems of *Sagesse*, written after his release from prison in January 1875, lack the anxious, questioning note that characterises the earlier poems in the volume. Verlaine tends, instead, to adopt an intellectual approach to his new situation, examining various facets of it, proclaiming his firm determination to resist temptation, looking for historical precedents for his religious ardour and expressing views on contemporary religious and political problems.

As in earlier volumes, there are therefore two kinds of poetry in *Sagesse*; on the one hand the poems written in 1873 and 1874 when Verlaine was under the stress first of his quarrel with Rimbaud, then of his arrest and trial, and finally of his return to Catholicism; on the other hand the poems written from 1875 onwards when Verlaine, secure in his new-found, or rediscovered faith, tended to lapse, as at the time of *La Bonne Chanson*, into a descriptive and analytical kind of verse.

These two different kinds of poetry are handled, as in previous volumes, in two different styles. The earlier poems are marked by a certain simplicity and directness, an absence of rhetorical devices and an impression of casualness and spontaneity that is reminiscent of the best poetry of the preceding volumes. In 'Je ne sais pourquoi . . .', once one has accepted the image of the poet's soul as a seagull being buffeted by the waves, the syntax has that simplicity that has been noted in *Poèmes saturniens* as Verlaine adds one phrase to another in a seemingly 'uncomposed' way, with an apparently casual repetition, or near-repetition, of the first and last lines of certain stanzas:

> Je ne sais pourquoi
> Mon esprit amer
> D'une aile inquiète et folle vole sur la mer.
> Tout ce qui m'est cher,
> D'une aile d'effroi
> Mon amour le couve au ras des flots. Pourquoi, pourquoi?

> Mouette à l'essor mélancolique
> Elle suit la vague, ma pensée,
> A tous les vents du ciel balancée
> Et biaisant quand la marée oblique,
> Mouette à l'essor mélancolique . . .

> Parfois si tristement elle crie
> Qu'elle alarme au lointain le pilote,
> Puis au gré du vent se livre et flotte
> Et plonge, et l'aile toute meurtrie
> Revole, et puis si tristement crie . . .

Similarly, in 'Le ciel est, par-dessus le toit . . .' the third line of
each verse is almost, but not quite, a repetition of the first line of
each verse, and the vocabulary and syntax are extremely simple
and even familiar, particularly in the last stanza:

> Le ciel est, par-dessus le toit,
>> Si bleu, si calme!
> Un arbre, par-dessus le toit,
>> Berce sa palme.
>
> La cloche, dans le ciel qu'on voit,
>> Doucement tinte.
> Un oiseau sur l'arbre qu'on voit
>> Chante sa plainte.
>
> Mon Dieu, mon Dieu, la vie est là,
>> Simple et tranquille.
> Cette paisible rumeur-là
>> Vient de la ville.
>
> —Qu'as-tu fait, ô toi que voilà
>> Pleurant sans cesse,
> Dis, qu'as-tu fait, toi que voilà,
>> De ta jeunesse?

'Un grand sommeil noir . . .', dated, in *Cellulairement*, 8 August
1873, the day of the trial, expresses in the simplest possible terms
the overwhelming sense of grief Verlaine must have felt when
sentence was passed on him:

> Un grand sommeil noir
> Tombe sur ma vie:
> Dormez, tout espoir,
> Dormez toute envie!
>
> Je ne vois plus rien,
> Je perds la mémoire
> Du mal et du bien . . .
> O la triste histoire!
>
> Je suis un berceau
> Qu'une main balance
> Au creux d'un caveau:
> Silence, silence!

In its companion poem, 'L'espoir luit . . .', written almost certainly just before the unsuccessful appeal of 27 August,[18]

although Verlaine uses the formal structure of a sonnet in alexandrines for the first time since *Poèmes saturniens*, he succeeds in
damping down any declamatory tone by using short, simple sentences and by making no attempt to avoid repeating, in an irregular and apparently careless way, the same, or related words
and phrases—'l'espoir luit comme un brin de paille dans l'ét-
able', 'l'espoir luit comme un caillou dans un creux', 'pauvre
âme pâle', 'pauvres malheureux', 'que ne t'endormais-tu', 'dors
après', 'il dort', 'va, dors':

> L'espoir luit comme un brin de paille dans l'étable.
> Que crains-tu de la guêpe ivre de son vol fou?
> Vois, le soleil toujours poudroie à quelque trou.
> Que ne t'endormais-tu, le coude sur la table?
>
> Pauvre âme pâle, au moins cette eau de puits glacé,
> Bois-la. Puis dors après. Allons, tu vois, je reste,
> Et je dorloterai les rêves de ta sieste,
> Et tu chantonneras comme un enfant bercé.
>
> Midi sonne. De grâce, éloignez-vous, madame.
> Il dort. C'est étonnant comme les pas de femme
> Résonnent au cerveau des pauvres malheureux.
>
> Midi sonne. J'ai fait arroser dans la chambre.
> Va, dors! L'espoir luit comme un caillou dans un creux.
> Ah! quand refleuriront les roses de septembre!

The same kind of style can be detected in the dialogue between
the poet and God which, although it is a sequence of ten sonnets
in alexandrines, is simply founded on the first commandment:
'Mon Dieu m'a dit: "Mon fils, il faut m'aimer" . . .' This is
then repeated with increasing insistency throughout the 140 lines
of the poem with Verlaine repeatedly protesting that he dare not
respond to this commandment. This simplicity of the overall
structure is accompanied by a simplicity of syntax even more
marked than in 'Je ne sais pourquoi . . .' as Verlaine strings
phrases along one after the other in an apparently spontaneous
fashion:

> Mon Dieu m'a dit: 'Mon fils, il faut m'aimer. Tu vois
> Mon flanc percé, mon cœur qui rayonne et qui saigne,
> Et mes pieds offensés que Madeleine baigne
> De larmes, et mes bras, douloureux sous le poids

De tes péchés, et mes mains! Et tu vois la croix,
Tu vois les clous, le fiel, l'éponge, et tout t'enseigne
A n'aimer, en ce monde amer où la chair règne,
Que ma Chair et mon Sang, ma parole et ma voix . . .

J'ai répondu: 'Seigneur, vous avez dit mon âme,
C'est vrai que je vous cherche et ne vous trouve pas.
Mais vous aimer! Voyez comme je suis en bas,
Vous dont l'amour toujours monte comme la flamme,

Vous, la source de paix que toute soif réclame,
Hélas! voyez un peu tous mes tristes combats . . .

—Aime-moi! Ces deux mots sont mes verbes suprêmes,
Car étant ton Dieu tout puissant, je peux *vouloir*,
Mais je ne veux d'abord que *pouvoir* que tu m'aimes . . .

—Seigneur, j'ai peur. Mon âme en moi tressaille toute.
Je vois, je sens qu'il faut vous aimer: mais comment
Moi, ceci, me ferai-je, ô Vous, Dieu, votre amant . . .

—Je te ferai goûter sur terre mes prémices,
La paix du cœur, l'amour d'être pauvre, et mes soirs
Mystiques, quand l'esprit s'ouvre aux calmes espoirs
Et croit boire, suivant ma promesse, au Calice
Eternel . . .

—Ah! Seigneur, qu'ai-je? Hélas, me voici tout en larmes
D'une joie extraordinaire! votre voix
Me fait comme du bien et du mal à la fois,
Et le mal et le bien, tout a les mêmes charmes . . .

J'ai l'extase et j'ai la terreur d'être choisi.
Je suis indigne, mais je sais votre clémence,
Ah! quel effort, mais quelle ardeur! Et me voici

Plein d'une humble prière, encor qu'un trouble immense
Brouille l'espoir que votre voix me révéla,
Et j'aspire en tremblant . . .
                              —Pauvre âme, c'est cela.

This directness and simplicity are still apparent in some of the poems Verlaine wrote after his conversion and after his release from prison in January 1875, notably when he looked back on what had occurred and re-lived the emotions he had experienced. In the opening poem of *Sagesse*, for example, 'Bon chevalier masqué . . .', probably written in the summer of 1875, he describes the misfortune of his imprisonment and the good fortune of his consequent conversion through the child-like allegory of a knight in armour first thrusting a lance through his heart and then giving him new life. The naïve quality of this fairy-tale atmosphere is enhanced by the simple rhyming couplets, each one of which forms a short, uncomplicated sentence, and by the quasi-spontaneous effect created by the irregular repetitions—'mon vieux cœur' is repeated three times in the first three couplets, on each occasion in a different place, and is later echoed by 'tout un cœur pur et fier' and 'tout un cœur jeune et bon':

> Bon chevalier masqué qui chevauche en silence,
> Le malheur a percé mon vieux cœur de sa lance.
>
> Le sang de mon vieux cœur n'a fait qu'un jet vermeil,
> Puis s'est évaporé sur les fleurs, au soleil.
>
> L'ombre éteignit mes yeux, un cri vint à ma bouche,
> Et mon vieux cœur est mort dans un frisson farouche.
>
> Alors le chevalier Malheur s'est rapproché,
> Il a mis pied à terre et sa main m'a touché.
>
> Son doigt ganté de fer entra dans ma blessure
> Tandis qu'il attestait sa loi d'une voix dure.
>
> Et voici qu'au contact glacé du doigt de fer
> Un cœur me renaissait, tout un cœur pur et fier.
>
> Et voici que, fervent d'une candeur divine,
> Tout un cœur jeune et bon battit dans ma poitrine . . .

Somewhat similar characteristics can be perceived in another poem written in 1875 on an occasion when Verlaine had come close to yielding to temptation. Again a simple metaphor is used, that of a summer storm beating down the ripening crops, with the blue sky giving way to a blood red sunset lit by shafts of lightning. Again the sentences are short and uncomplicated and again there is the 'uncomposed' effect of the repetitions of the verb 'luire' and the expression 'ma pauvre âme', while the anxious, questioning note of the tercets is like an echo from the uncertain, troubled Verlaine of an earlier period:

> Les faux beaux jours ont lui tout le jour, ma pauvre âme,
> Et les voici vibrer aux cuivres du couchant.

Ferme les yeux, pauvre âme, et rentre sur-le-champ;
Une tentation des pires. Fuis l'Infâme.

Ils ont lui tout le jour en longs grêlons de flamme,
Battant toute vendange aux collines, couchant
Toute moisson de la vallée, et ravageant
Le ciel tout bleu, le ciel chanteur qui te réclame.

O pâlis, et va-t-en, lente et joignant les mains.
Si ces hiers allaient manger nos beaux demains?
Si la vieille folie était encore en route?

Ces souvenirs, va-t-il falloir les retuer?
Un assaut furieux, le suprême sans doute!
O, va prier contre l'orage, va prier.

Yet another poem from the summer of 1875 has the same kind of
theme as Verlaine pushes aside the temptations of everyday life.
Again the phrases are strung along one after the other as if he is
thinking aloud and as if, in fact, these temptations are coming
sweeping back once he has released the floodgates of memory—
the beauty of women, their weakness, their hands, their eyes,
above all their voices, whether consoling or concealing, whether
summoning or singing, whether calling or crying:

Beauté des femmes, leur faiblesse, et ces mains pâles
Qui font souvent le bien et peuvent tout le mal,
Et ces yeux, où plus rien ne reste d'animal
Que juste assez pour dire: 'assez' aux fureurs mâles,

Et toujours, maternelle endormeuse des râles,
Même quand elle ment, cette voix! Matinal
Appel, ou chant bien doux à vêpre, ou frais signal,
Ou beau sanglot qui va mourir au pli des châles . . .

But perhaps because these memories are having a different effect
from what he had intended Verlaine turns, in the tercets, after a
single line condemning the harshness of men and the ugliness of
life on earth, towards the life of innocence and tenderness that he
envisages after death, with a questioning note again being
introduced in the final lines:

Hommes durs! Vie atroce et laide d'ici-bas!
Ah! que du moins, loin des baisers et des combats,
Quelque chose demeure un peu sur la montagne,

> Quelque chose du cœur enfantin et subtil,
> Bonté, respect! Car qu'est-ce qui nous accompagne,
> Et vraiment, quand la mort viendra, que reste-t-il?

The directness and simplicity of these poems connected with the break with Rimbaud, the trial, the conversion and the early struggles against temptation, give way, however, to a more involved and elaborate style in other poems dating from the later months of 1875. The second poem of the volume, for example, is concerned, like 'Les faux beaux jours . . .' and 'Beauté des femmes . . .' with the temptations of the flesh. But this time Verlaine uses a wealth of comparisons to describe his efforts, although his erudite accumulation of classical references is far less convincing than the single, simple metaphors of the other two poems:

> J'avais peiné comme Sisyphe
> Et comme Hercule travaillé
> Contre la Chair qui se rebiffe,
>
> J'avais lutté, j'avais baillé
> Des coups à trancher des montagnes,
> Et comme Achille ferraillé . . .
>
> Que ma chance fût male ou bonne,
> Toujours un parti de mon cœur
> Ouvrait sa porte à la Gorgone . . .

The same objection can be made to the last poem of the first section of *Sagesse*, in which Verlaine tries to distinguish between different forms of maternal sorrow and contrasts the two classical examples of Hecuba, Queen of Troy, and Niobe, Queen of Phrygia, with the Virgin Mary. But this kind of intellectual discussion is ill-suited to Verlaine's particular poetic gifts and the poem is prosaic in the extreme:

> L'âme antique était rude et vaine,
> Et ne voyait dans la douleur
> Que l'acuité de la peine
> Ou l'étonnement du malheur.
>
> L'art, sa figure la plus claire,
> Traduit ce double sentiment
> Par deux grands types de la Mère
> En proie au suprême tourment.

> C'est la vieille reine de Troie;
> Tous ses fils sont morts par le fer . . .

> Et c'est Niobé, qui s'effare
> Et garde fixement des yeux
> Sur les dalles de pierre rare
> Ses enfants tués par les dieux . . .

> La douleur chrétienne est immense,
> Elle, comme le cœur humain;
> Elle souffre, puis elle pense,
> Et calme poursuit son chemin.

> Elle est debout sur le Calvaire
> Pleine de larmes et sans cris.
> C'est également une Mère,
> Mais quelle Mère de quel Fils! . . .

Other specifically religious poems adopt the same analytical approach and the second one in the second section of *Sagesse*, in which Verlaine expresses his love for the Virgin Mary, is strongly reminiscent of those poems of *La Bonne Chanson* in which he also promised to mend his ways, for love of Mathilde Mauté:

> Je ne veux plus aimer que ma mère Marie.
> Tous les autres amours sont de commandement.
> Nécessaires qu'ils sont, ma mère seulement
> Pourra les allumer aux cœurs qui l'ont chérie.

> C'est pour Elle qu'il faut chérir mes ennemis,
> C'est par Elle que j'ai voué ce sacrifice,
> Et la douceur de cœur et le zèle au service,
> Comme je la priais, Elle les a permis.

> Et comme j'étais faible et bien méchant encore,
> Aux mains lâches, les yeux éblouis des chemins,
> Elle baissa mes yeux et me joignit les mains,
> Et m'enseigna les mots par lesquels on adore . . .

A similar kind of technique can be seen in the twin sonnets 'Sagesse d'un Louis Racine . . .' and 'Non, il fut gallican, ce siècle . . .', in which Verlaine turns to the seventeenth century, in the former poem, and to the Middle Ages, in the latter poem, to find a faith akin to his own. In their cataloguing of the joys of life in France towards the end of the reign of Louis XIV:

> Quand Maintenon jetait sur la France ravie
> L'ombre douce et la paix de ses coiffes de lin,

> Et royale abritait la veuve et l'orphelin,
> Quand l'étude de la prière était suivie,
>
> Quand poète et docteur, simplement, bonnement,
> Communiaient avec des ferveurs de novices,
> Humbles servaient la Messe et chantaient aux offices . . .

and of the multiple careers open to mediaeval man:

> Roi, politicien, moine, artisan, chimiste,
> Architecte, soldat, médecin, avocat,
> Quel temps! Oui, que mon cœur naufragé rembarquât
> Pour toute cette force ardente, souple, artiste . . .

these lines are far removed indeed from the poetry of the *Ariettes oubliées* in *Romances sans Paroles* and of the half-dozen poems written in prison in 1873 and 1874 which are included in *Sagesse*. But it is when dealing not with past history but with contemporary history that Verlaine, whose religious conversion had been accompanied by a political conversion to Royalism, lapses into an even more painfully prosaic kind of verse, as in the two poems, probably written late in 1875 and in 1879 respectively, attacking those holding rationalist and Republican convictions. The first of these poems, with its involved syntax, its heavy sarcasm and its vague allusion to a recent Republican victory, probably that of 1875 when the Constitution of the Third Republic was finally decided, is a barely readable 'pièce de médiocre polémique', as one critic has described it[19]:

> Petits amis qui sûtes nous prouver
> Par A plus B que deux et deux font quatre,
> Mais qui depuis voulez parachever
> Une victoire où l'on se laissait battre,
>
> Et couronner vos conquêtes d'un coup
> Par ce soufflet à la mémoire humaine:
> 'Dieu ne nous a révélé rien du tout
> Car nous disons qu'il n'est que l'ombre vaine,
>
> Que le profil et que l'allongement
> Sur tous les murs que la peur édifie
> De votre pur et simple mouvement,
> Et nous dictons cette philosophie' . . .

The second one, written some time later after an electoral victory by the Republican party, suffers from the same faults:

Or, vous voici promus, petits amis,
  Depuis les temps de ma lettre première,
Promus, disais-je, aux fiers emplois promis
  A votre thèse, en ces jours de lumière.

Vous voici rois de France! A votre tour!
  (Rois à plusieurs d'une France postiche,
Mais rois de fait et non sans quelque amour
  D'un trône lourd avec un budget riche . . .

These clumsy attacks on the Republicans are complemented by a painfully sentimental defence of the Jesuits which Verlaine wrote on the occasion of their expulsion from one of their houses in 1880:

Vous reviendrez bientôt, les bras pleins de pardons
  Selon votre coutume,
O Pères excellents qu'aujourd'hui nous perdons
  Pour comble d'amertume.

Vous reviendrez, vieillards exquis, avec l'honneur,
  Avec la Fleur chérie,
Et que de pleurs joyeux, et quels cris de bonheur
  Dans toute la patrie . . .

An even worse example of this kind of exaggerated sentimentality is the poem Verlaine wrote on hearing the news of the death of the Prince Imperial, the son of the former Emperor Napoleon III, in 1879, for in spite of his wish to see the Royalist symbol of the 'fleur de lys' return to France along with Catholicism, his hatred of secular Republicanism was so intense that he would have preferred Bonapartism as an alternative:

Prince mort en soldat à cause de la France,
  Ame certes élue,
Fier jeune homme si pur tombé plein d'espérance,
  Je t'aime et te salue! . . .

Et je dis, réservant d'ailleurs mon vœu suprême
  Au lys de Louis Seize:
Napoléon, qui fus digne du diadème,
  Gloire à ta mort française . . .

Verlaine was, however, still capable of reverting at times to the manner of the earlier poems of *Sagesse* under the impact of a deeply felt emotion. In 1878, for example, he was allowed to visit his six-year-old son Georges and, of the four poems inspired by this momentary renewal of family ties, one at least has something of the authentic Verlainian note, particularly in the opening stanza with its simple appeal to Mathilde, its short, octosyllabic lines and its feminine rhymes throughout:

> Ecoutez la chanson bien douce
> Qui ne pleure que pour vous plaire.
> Elle est discrète, elle est légère:
> Un frisson d'eau sur de la mousse . . .

The same might be said of one of its companion poems about Mathilde's hands, which is also in octosyllabic lines and exclusively feminine rhymes:

> Les chères mains qui furent miennes,
> Toutes petites, toutes belles,
> Après ces méprises mortelles
> Et toutes ces choses païennes . . .

But the other two poems of the group, 'On n'offense que Dieu qui seule pardonne . . .' and 'Et j'ai revu l'enfant unique . . .' are lacking in any such simplicity and directness, as they are in the octosyllabic rhythm and the feminine rhymes throughout. Both are in conventionally rhymed alexandrines and both have the now familiar defects of going into too much detail, padding out the phrasing and using banal imagery, as in the following lines where Verlaine's good resolutions are reminiscent of those he made in *La Bonne Chanson*:

> Alors un grand désir, un seul, vient investir
> Le pénitent, après les premières alarmes,
> Et c'est d'humilier son front devant les larmes
> De naguère, sans rien qui pourrait amortir
> Le coup droit pour l'orgueil, et de rendre les armes
> Comme un soldat vaincu,—triste, de bonne foi . . .

The second of the two poems uses the same image of the wounded heart that Verlaine had used three years before in 'Bon chevalier masqué . . .'. But whereas those lines, with their quasi-spontaneous effect and characteristically irregular repetition were simply and even naïvely descriptive, the later poem defines and analyses in a laborious and painstaking way that makes the sense difficult to follow and deprives the poem of any emotional impact:

> Et j'ai revu l'enfant unique: il m'a semblé
> Que s'ouvrait dans mon cœur la dernière blessure,
> Celle dont la douleur plus exquise m'assure
> D'une mort désirable en un jour consolé.
>
> La bonne flèche aigüe et sa fraîcheur qui dure!
> En ces instants choisis elles ont éveillé
> Les rêves un peu lourds du scrupule ennuyé,
> Et tout mon sang chrétien chanta la Chanson pure . . .

The landscapes which form such a substantial part of *Sagesse* and to which Verlaine readily turned his hand during his years in England from 1875 to 1877 are scarcely any better. On occasions the old 'impair' rhythm returns and one or two poems have a not unsuccessful opening verse, such as this description of the flat landscape of Lincolnshire:

> L'échelonnement des haies
> Moutonne à l'infini, mer
> Claire dans le brouillard clair
> Qui sent bon les jeunes baies.

But inspiration then seems to flag and the second and third verses become something of a catalogue and include one particularly awkward rhyme that Verlaine in his earlier days would certainly have avoided:

> Des arbres et des moulins
> Sont légers sur le vert tendre
> Où vient s'ébattre et s'étendre
> L'agilité des poulains.
>
> Dans ce vague d'un Dimanche
> Voici se jouer aussi
> De grandes brebis aussi
> Douces que leur laine blanche . . .

The landscapes he describes during his holiday periods in northern France are even duller. The poem 'Parisien, mon frère . . .' incorporates the desperately prosaic line: 'Montons. Il fait si frais encor, montons encor', before launching into a minutely detailed account of Arras seen from the surrounding hills, like a stage setting viewed from a theatre balcony:

Là! nous voilà 'placés' comme dans une 'loge
De face'; et le 'décor' vraiment tire un éloge:
La cathédrale énorme et le beffroi sans fin,
Ces toits de tuile sous ces verdures, le vain
Appareil des remparts pompeux et grands quand même,
Ces clochers, cette tour, ces autres, sur l'or blême
Des nuages à l'ouest . . .

All too many of the later poems of *Sagesse*, written between
1875 and 1880 tend to be of this kind, laboriously composed with
none of the emotional content that distinguishes the language of
poetry from the language of what Mallarmé called 'l'universel
reportage'.[20]

This kind of poem also occurs of course during the earlier
period in prison, as it had done throughout Verlaine's life and in
nearly all his previous volumes of verse. But when he abandoned
his idea of publishing under the title *Cellulairement* the poems he
had written in prison, he held back, for volumes to be published
after *Sagesse*, the narrative and descriptive kind of poem, and of
the thirty-two poems originally intended for *Cellulairement* he included only seven in *Sagesse*, 'Je ne sais pourquoi . . .', 'Un grand
sommeil noir . . .', 'Je suis venu, calme orphelin . . .', 'La bise se
rue . . .', 'L'espoir luit . . .', 'Du fond du grabat . . .', and the
sonnet sequence 'Mon Dieu m'a dit . . .', all of which have that
note of anxiety and that simplicity of expression which characterises the best of Verlaine's poetry.

These seven poems also have, for the most part, the kind of
versification that is characteristically Verlainian. Three of them,
'Je ne sais pourquoi . . .', 'Un grand sommeil noir . . .' and 'Du
fond du grabat . . .' are in 'vers impairs' and two of them are in
octosyllabic lines, 'Je suis venu, calme orphelin . . .' and 'La bise
se rue . . .' Only 'L'espoir luit . . .' and the dialogue with God
are in alexandrines, as well as having the formal structure of the
sonnet, and it may well be that this reflects Verlaine's desire to
return to a stable and ordered existence. But even so, it is worthy
of note that, particularly in the dialogue, there is such an extensive use of 'enjambement' and the caesura is so frequently
displaced and even abolished altogether[21] that it is as if Verlaine
was as yet incapable of making a whole-hearted return to traditional forms. The following lines from the fourth sonnet, for

example, though technically alexandrines, have the fragmented rhythms of many of the *Romances sans Paroles*:

Seigneur, c'est trop! Vraiment je n'ose. Aimer qui? Vous?
Oh! non! Je tremble et n'ose. Oh! vous aimer, je n'ose,
Je ne veux pas! je suis indigne. Vous, la Rose
Immense des purs vents de l'Amour, ô Vous, tous

Les cœurs des Saints, ô Vous qui fûtes le Jaloux
D'Israël, Vous la chaste abeille qui se pose
Sur la seule fleur d'une Innocence mi-close,
Quoi, *moi, moi,* pouvoir *Vous* aimer . . .

Further evidence of this same inability to return entirely to traditional forms may be perceived in another poem, 'Parfums, couleurs, systèmes, lois . . .', written towards the end of 1874 (although, for some reason, not included in the projected *Cellulairement*) which is in the form of a sonnet, but an inverted sonnet, with the two tercets preceding the two quatrains, a form with which Verlaine had experimented in 'Résignation', the first poem of the section *Melancholia* of *Poèmes saturniens*, and in 'Le Bon Disciple' dated 'mai 1872' though never actually published by Verlaine.[22] Two other poems, also excluded from *Cellulairement* although written at the very beginning of the period covered by *Sagesse*, have equally typical Verlainian rhythms. 'Tournez, tournez, bons chevaux de bois . . .' in a slightly different version from the one included in *Romances sans Paroles*, retains the 'impair' line of nine syllables that it had in the earlier volume, and 'Le ciel est, par-dessus le toit . . .' written in July 1873 when Verlaine was first arrested, is in lines of eight and four syllables. In another poem it is the rhyme rather than the rhythm which has a typically Verlainian originality, reminiscent of 'C'est le chien de Jean de Nivelle . . .' in *Romances sans Paroles*. This is the sonnet 'Beauté des femmes . . .', quoted on p. 59 above, in which the quatrains give an impression of false rhymes in that both the masculine and feminine rhymes have the same sound—'pâles', 'mal', 'animal', 'mâles'; 'râles', 'matinal', 'signal', 'châles'. The vowel 'a' further recurs in two of the three rhymes in the tercets, 'bas', 'combats', 'montagne', 'subtil', 'accompagne', 'reste-t-il', and this unusual use of different rhymes based on the same vowel can also be seen in the sonnet 'Les faux beaux jours . . .' (see p. 59 above), where the rhymes 'âme', 'infâme', 'flamme' and 'réclame' are very close to their neighbouring rhymes 'couchant', 'champ', 'couchant' and 'ravageant'.

But in the poems of *Sagesse* written after Verlaine's return to Catholicism his more stable situation and more 'composed' style are usually matched by a more conventional kind of versification. Whereas four of the ten poems mentioned above as dating from 1873 and 1874 are in 'vers impairs' and four others partly or wholly in octosyllabic lines, with just two in alexandrines, of the remaining thirty-seven poems in the first edition of *Sagesse* only six are in 'vers impairs' and only five in octosyllabic lines. The vast majority are in the traditional twelve-syllable line so that, in the volume as a whole, the alexandrine, which had played such a reduced rôle in *Fêtes galantes* and *Romances sans Paroles*, and even *La Bonne Chanson*, makes an emphatic return in twenty poems, in addition to the dialogue, that is almost half the total, which is roughly the same proportion as in *Poèmes saturniens*. Similarly the sonnet which, after *Poèmes saturniens*, had completely disappeared from the three succeeding volumes, comes back into favour and is used in ten poems, in addition to the ten sonnets of the dialogue.

Along with this return to traditional patterns of rhyme and rhythm Verlaine also moves from the twilight atmosphere reminiscent of that of *Romances sans Paroles* towards a much lighter tone analogous to that which pervades *La Bonne Chanson*, and for very much the same reason in that, during this second period of stability and certainty it is only natural that Verlaine's poetry should again be bathed in sunlight rather than remain shadowed and overcast. 'Je ne veux plus aimer que ma mère Marie . . .', 'L'échelonnement des haies . . .', 'La mer est plus belle . . .', 'Parisien, mon frère . . .' and 'C'est la fête du blé . . .', all of them written from 1875 onwards, are typical of this lighter tonality and are in marked contrast to the darker atmosphere of the earlier poems, 'Le son du cor s'afflige vers le les bois . . .', 'Je ne sais pourquoi . . .', 'Un grand sommeil noir . . .' and 'L'espoir luit . . .'

In terms therefore of its content, its style, its versification and its tonality *Sagesse* may be said to be like a mirror image of *La*

Bonne Chanson and *Romances sans Paroles* taken together. That is to say that the early poems of *Sagesse* are, broadly speaking, contemporary with and of much the same inspiration as *Romances sans Paroles*; but as Verlaine emerges from this period of stress and conflict into a period of calm and stability he abandons his simple, unconventional and deeply moving kind of poetry and reverts to the formal, discursive and prosaic type of verse that he had written in *La Bonne Chanson*.

IV

THE MINOR POETRY

Jadis et Naguère

In the pious and penitent preface that Verlaine wrote for *Sagesse* in 1880 he referred to the sins that he had 'jadis et presque naguère pratiqués'. Four years later, in 1884, he made use of this phrase to form the title of his next volume of poetry which, however, scarcely deserved the second half of its title since no more than half a dozen poems were of recent date. The remainder belonged very much to 'jadis' rather than 'naguère', having been written more than ten years before. They can be broadly divided into three groups, (*a*) a verse play of some twenty pages, *Les uns et les autres*, written in 1871 and clearly intended as a 'fête galante' for the stage, with a costumed singer playing a mandoline and surrounded by gay young revellers going under such names as Corydon and Rosalinde, (*b*) some fifteen or so poems dating from an even earlier period, 1867–9, and (*c*) a similar number of poems written in prison in 1873 and 1874, most of them taken over from the abandoned *Cellulairement*. The *Naguère* section, which is less than half the size of the *Jadis* section, is in fact made up exclusively, except for a short prologue, of five fairly long poems from *Cellulairement*.

Since *Jadis et Naguère* is not therefore a new work but a rather heterogeneous collection of poems from previous periods, one might expect that, like the previous volumes, it too would reveal the two aspects of Verlaine's talent that are so noticeable in his earlier volumes. But unfortunately Verlaine had already creamed off the best of his poetry for those volumes and in consequence *Jadis et Naguère* is a decidedly second-rate piece of work. The poems that come nearest to the kind of quality that has been encountered in 'Soleils couchants', 'Colloque sentimental', 'La lune blanche . . .', 'Il pleure dans mon cœur . . .' and 'Je ne sais pourquoi . . .', to choose just one example from each of the five previous volumes, are, not surprisingly, those that were composed in 1873 and 1874. One such is 'Sonnet boiteux', given this title presumably because it is in 'vers impairs' with the unusual number of thirteen syllables to each line, but also perhaps because the two tercets do not observe the pattern of rhymes that is customary in a sonnet. In fact they do not observe any pattern of rhymes at all and are therefore written in blank verse, unless one argues that a rhyme is intended between 'Sohos' and 'haôs' and that there is assonance based on the vowel 'i' between 'glapit', 'triste' and 'Bible', leaving only 'espérance' without even a last vestige of a rhyme. Another irregularity too should be noted—namely that the first quatrain has masculine rhymes only and the second quatrain feminine rhymes only, which is the pattern Verlaine had used in 'Birds in the Night' and 'Tournez, tournez, bons chevaux de bois . . .', instead of the usual pattern of masculine and feminine rhymes within each stanza:

> Ah! vraiment c'est triste, ah! vraiment ça finit trop mal.
> Il n'est pas permis d'être à ce point infortuné.
> Ah! vraiment c'est trop la mort du naïf animal
> Qui voit tout son sang couler sous son regard fané.
>
> Londres fume et crie. O quelle ville de la Bible!
> Le gaz flambe et nage et les enseignes sont vermeilles.
> Et les maisons dans leur ratatinement terrible
> Epouvantent comme un sénat de petites vieilles.
>
> Tout l'affreux passé saute, piaule, miaule et glapit
> Dans le brouillard rose et jaune et sale des Sohos
> Avec des *indeeds* et des *all rights* et des *haôs*.
>
> Non vraiment c'est trop un martyre sans espérance,
> Non vraiment cela finit trop mal, vraiment c'est triste:
> O le feu du ciel sur cette ville de la Bible!

Although this condemnation by Verlaine of the life he had led in London with Rimbaud lacks the customary sad and melancholy note, creating instead an impression of extreme violence and impotent rage, it nevertheless deserves a high place in Verlaine's poetry for the way in which this mood, though unusual, is conveyed in characteristic fashion with a certain casualness of language and syntax. To English ears line 11 may sound rather contrived, but the poem as a whole, with its irregular repetitions, its exclamations, its quite ordinary verbs used in an extraordinary and evocative way and its restless rhythms gives powerful expression to Verlaine's feeling of bitter regret, during the early months of his imprisonment,[1] about the relationship between himself and Rimbaud, a relationship which is not made explicit in the poem but is merely implied in the imprecation of the final line. It is a poem which, in terms of its quality, should have found a place in *Sagesse* but Verlaine no doubt felt that the subject was unsuitable.

It was certainly for this reason that Verlaine excluded another poem concerned with Rimbaud, 'Vers pour être calomnié', since this was included in the first manuscript of *Sagesse* where it is crossed out. Like 'Sonnet boiteux' it is a sonnet in 'vers impairs', but this time of eleven syllables, and it has a similar irregularity in the rhyme scheme in that the first quatrain is in exclusively masculine rhymes and the second quatrain in exclusively feminine rhymes. But there is a further irregularity in that the same two rhymes are used in both quatrains, so that there is an impression of false rhymes between the masculine rhymes of the first quatrain and the feminine rhymes of the second. In the tercets, moreover, there is an actual false rhyme between 'tel' in line 11 and 'immortelle' in line 14:

> Ce soir je m'étais penché sur ton sommeil.
> Tout ton corps dormait chaste sur l'humble lit,
> Et j'ai vu, comme un qui s'applique et qui lit,
> Ah! j'ai vu que tout est vain sous le soleil!
>
> Qu'on vive, ô quelle délicate merveille,
> Tant notre appareil est une fleur qui plie!
> O pensée aboutissant à la folie!
> Va, pauvre, dors! moi, l'effroi pour toi m'éveille.
>
> Ah! misère de t'aimer, mon frêle amour
> Qui vas respirant comme on expire un jour!
> O regard fermé que la mort fera tel!
>
> O bouche qui ris en songe sur ma bouche,
> En attendant l'autre rire plus farouche!
> Vite, éveille-toi. Dis, l'âme est immortelle?

These experiments with rhyme are reminiscent of *Romances sans Paroles*, where the sixth of the *Ariettes oubliées*, 'C'est le chien de Jean de Nivelle . . .', has false rhymes throughout (see p. 48 above) and of 'Beauté des femmes . . .' in *Sagesse* where the masculine and feminine rhymes in the quatrains have the same sound (see p. 59 above). But although the poem was clearly written during the period 1872–3 when Verlaine and Rimbaud were living together, its subject no doubt made it as unsuitable for inclusion in *Romances sans Paroles* as in *Sagesse*. As far as its mood is concerned, however, it would have been eminently suitable for inclusion in either volume, since it expresses the profound disquiet which recurs in Rimbaud's *Une Saison en Enfer* where, in the section 'Vierge folle—l'Époux infernal' of the chapter 'Délires', he puts into the mouth of his 'foolish virgin' the following words, very close to those of Verlaine's own sonnet:

A côté de son cher corps endormi, que d'heures des nuits j'ai veillé, cherchant pourquoi il voulait tant s'évader de la réalité . . .

The passage 'Vagabonds' of Rimbaud's *Illuminations* should also be read as a comment on Verlaine's poem:

Pitoyable frère, que d'atroces veillées je lui dus! . . . presque chaque nuit, aussitôt endormi, le pauvre frère se levait, la bouche pourrie, les yeux arrachés—tel qu'il se rêvait!—et me tirait dans la salle en hurlant son songe de chagrin idiot . . .

Not only the versification and the mood of the sonnet are typical of Verlaine at the height of his powers in 1872–3 but its style too is characteristic of the best Verlaine with a simplicity of syntax and a refusal to analyse or explain so that the profound feeling of fear and anxiety comes over in what might be called a pure state.

A third poem of *Jadis et Naguère* which deserves particular attention is 'Crimen Amoris', the first of the five 'récits diaboliques', as Verlaine called them, which make up the 'Naguère' section of the volume. It too was written in 'vers impairs' of eleven syllables and also dates from 1873, shortly after Verlaine's arrest when the disquiet expressed in 'Vers pour être calomnié' had developed into a total rejection of Rimbaud's ideas. One of these ideas, that lay at the very basis of Rimbaud's philosophy, was the notion of 'l'amour universel', including the homosexual love which undoubtedly existed between the two poets, as 'Vers pour être calomnié' amply proves. But, as has been seen, this latter poem equally proves that Verlaine was never entirely in sympathy with Rimbaud's ideas and that his Christian upbringing had left him with nagging doubts and fears that he was unable to throw off as readily as Rimbaud. After the quarrel between the two poets and Verlaine's arrest these doubts and fears crystallised, as has been seen in 'Sonnet boiteux', and even before his conversion Verlaine returned to a Christian standpoint, as he conceived it, and decided that Rimbaud's ideas were wrong and that 'l'amour universel' was a crime—hence the title 'Crimen Amoris'.

At first sight the poem appears to belong to the discursive kind in that it has a clear 'story line' and gives a vivid account of demons celebrating the festival of the seven sins in Hell. The handsomest of these demons 'avait seize ans sous sa couronne de fleurs' and is clearly Rimbaud. He climbs to the top of the highest tower of the infernal palace and announces that the struggle between good and evil is over and that he is going to sacrifice Hell to the new concept of universal love. He thereupon hurls down the torch he holds in his hand and the palace bursts into flames with the demons singing as they die. But suddenly there is a tremendous roll of thunder which puts an end to the singing and indicates that the sacrifice has not been accepted and that 'quelqu'un de fort et de juste assurément' has intervened. The poem ends with the infernal palace fading like a dream and being replaced by 'une campagne évangélique' awaiting the arrival of 'Le Dieu clément qui nous gardera du mal'.

Quite apart from the interest of the ideas expressed in the poem it is an impressive piece of work not because it is typically Verlainian in its manner, but because it is typically Rimbaldian, as if Verlaine had borrowed not only Rimbaud's ideas but Rimbaud's style as well. From the very beginning it has that colourful, exotic quality that one associates with Rimbaud:

> Dans un palais, soie et or, dans Ecbatane,
> De beaux démons, des Satans adolescents,
> Au son d'une musique mahométane
> Font litière aux Sept Péchés de leurs cinq sens.
>
> C'est la fête aux Sept Péchés: ô qu'elle est belle!
> Tous les Désirs rayonnaient en feux brutaux!
> Les Appétits, pages prompts que l'on harcèle,
> Promenaient des vins roses dans des cristaux . . .

The brilliant diamond-like glitter of Rimbaud's language in, for example, 'Le Bateau ivre' and even more so in passages from the *Illuminations* such as 'Mystique' and 'Barbare' is even more apparent later in the poem:

> La torche tombe de sa main éployée,
> Et l'incendie alors hurla s'élevant,
> Querelle énorme d'aigles rouges noyée
> Au remous noir de la fumée et du vent.
>
> L'or fond et coule à flots et le marbre éclate;
> C'est un brasier tout splendeur et tout ardeur;
> La soie en courts frissons comme de l'ouate
> Vole à flocons tout ardeur et tout splendeur . . .

This powerful, vivid poetry is quite untypical of Verlaine, but the end of the poem, on the other hand, after the rejection of Rimbaud's attempt to abolish the concept of good and evil, becomes much more characteristically Verlainian:

> Et c'est la nuit, la nuit bleue aux mille étoiles;
> Une campagne évangélique s'étend
> Sévère et douce, et, vagues comme des voiles,
> Les branches d'arbre ont l'air d'ailes s'agitant.
>
> De froids ruisseaux courent sur un lit de pierre;
> Les doux hiboux nagent vaguement dans l'air
> Tout embaumé de mystère et de prière;
> Parfois un flot qui saute lance un éclair.
>
> La forme molle au loin monte des collines
> Comme un amour encore mal défini,
> Et le brouillard qui s'essore des ravines
> Semble un effort vers quelque but réuni.
>
> Et tout cela comme un cœur et comme une âme,
> Et comme un verbe, et d'un amour virginal,
> Adore, s'ouvre en une extase et réclame
> Le Dieu clément qui nous gardera du mal.

Despite its discursive structure and despite the exceptional nature of the earlier imagery, the poem is characteristic of the best of Verlaine's poetry in that it does not merely tell a story but also puts across an emotion with telling effect. When Verlaine describes the festival of the Seven Sins this is not superfluous detail but conveys what he himself felt when swept away by Rimbaud's ideas:

> Des danses sur des rhythmes d'épithalames
> Bien doucement se pâmaient en longs sanglots
> Et de beaux chœurs de voix d'hommes et de femmes
> Se déroulaient, palpitaient comme des flots,
>
> Et la bonté qui s'en allait de ces choses
> Etait puissante et charmante tellement
> Que la campagne autour se fleurit de roses
> Et que la nuit paraissait en diamant . . .

And his magnificent portrait of Rimbaud conveys a tremendous impression of the admiration he felt for the latter's powerful personality allied to a strange tenderness towards him:

> Or le plus beau d'entre tous ces mauvais anges
> Avait seize ans sous sa couronne de fleurs.
> Les bras croisés sur les colliers et les franges,
> Il rêve, l'œil plein de flammes et de pleurs.
>
> En vain la fête autour se faisait plus folle,
> En vain les Satans, ses frères et ses sœurs,
> Pour l'arracher au souci qui le désole,
> L'encourageaient d'appels de bras caresseurs:
>
> Il résistait à toutes câlineries,
> Et le chagrin mettait un papillon noir
> A son cher front tout brûlant d'orfèvreries.
> O l'immortel et terrible désespoir! . . .

It is this that distinguishes 'Crimen Amoris' from the other four 'récits diaboliques', 'La Grâce', 'L'Impénitence finale', 'Don Juan pipé' and 'Amoureuse du Diable' which are simply rather long, involved and frankly boring, if slightly blood-curdling tales on the theme of death and damnation. One has to go right back to a poem such as 'La Mort de Philippe II' in *Poèmes saturniens* to find something of the same sort in Verlaine's work and it has indeed been suggested by one critic that these 'récits' are in fact early works which Verlaine polished up during his enforced leisure in prison.[2] On balance, this seems unlikely in view of the fact that 'Don Juan pipé', for example, has exactly the same theme as 'Crimen Amoris'—the rebel against God who is punished for his rebellion. There are even certain similarities of setting and of language, as when Don Juan, cast down into hell, raises the standard of revolt among the damned:

> Le grand damné, royal sous ses haillons,
> Promène autour son œil plein de rayons,
> Et crie: 'A moi l'Enfer! ô vous qui fûtes
> Par moi guidés en vos sublimes chutes,
> Disciples de Don Juan, reconnaissez
> Ici la voix qui vous a redressés.
> Satan est mort, Dieu mourra dans la fête!
> Aux armes pour la suprême conquête!...

These lines bear a clear resemblance to the appeal launched from the topmost tower of hell by 'le plus beau d'entre tous les mauvais anges' in 'Crimen Amoris':

> Qu'est-ce qu'il dit de sa voix profonde et tendre
> Qui se marie au claquement clair du feu
> Et que la lune est extatique d'entendre?
> 'Oh! je serai celui-là qui créera Dieu!
>
> Nous avons tous trop souffert, anges et hommes,
> De ce conflit entre le Pire et le Mieux.
> Humilions, misérables que nous sommes,
> Tous nos élans dans le plus simple des vœux...
>
> Et pour réponse à Jésus qui crut bien faire
> En maintenant l'équilibre de ce duel,
> Par moi l'enfer, dont c'est ici le repaire
> Se sacrifie à l'Amour universel!'...

But if the ideas expressed in the two poems are the same, the quality of the poetry is different. This can be seen in the two passages quoted, but it emerges even more clearly when one reads the opening lines of 'Don Juan pipé' with their excess of superfluous detail:

> Don Juan, qui fut un grand Seigneur en ce monde,
> Est aux enfers ainsi qu'un pauvre immonde,
> Pauvre, sans la barbe faite, et pouilleux,
> Et si ce n'étaient la lueur de ses yeux
> Et la beauté de sa maigre figure,
> En le voyant ainsi quiconque jure
> Qu'il est un gueux et non ce héros fier,

Aux dames comme aux poètes si cher
Et dont l'auteur de ces humbles chroniques
Vous va parler sur des faits authentiques . . .

The same remarks can be made about 'La Grâce'. It too has a theme somewhat similar to that of 'Crimen Amoris' underlying the very different subject of a woman resisting the attempts of her husband, who has died in a state of mortal sin, to persuade her to join him in hell. But it too goes into far too much detail, as in the description of the severed head of the dead Count Henry being picked up by the Countess:

La Comtesse est debout, paumes épanouies.
Elle fait le grand cri des amours surhumains,
Puis se penche et saisit avec ses pâles mains
La tête qui, merveille, a l'aspect de sourire.
Un fantôme de vie et de chair semble luire
Sur le hideux objet qui rayonne à présent
Dans un nimbe languissamment phosphorescent.
Un halo clair, semblable à des cheveux d'aurore
Tremble au sommet et semble au vent flotter encore
Parmi le chant des cors à travers la forêt.
Les noirs orbites ont des éclairs, on dirait
De grands regards de flamme et noirs. Le trou farouche
Au rire affreux, qui fut, Comte Henry, votre bouche
Se transfigure rouge aux deux arcs palpitants
De lèvres qu'auréole un duvet de vingt ans,
Et qui pour un baiser se tendent savoureuses . . .

'L'Impénitence finale', as the title suggests, is very close in theme to 'Don Juan pipé' and 'Crimen Amoris' although, like 'La Grâce', it is a feminine rather than a masculine subject and concerns a woman who refuses to repent and out of whose consequent death Verlaine wrings the maximum amount of pathos:

O ses paupières violettes!
O ses petites mains qui tremblent, maigrelettes!
O tout son corps perdu dans les draps étouffants!
Regardez, elle meurt de la mort des enfants.
Et le prêtre anxieux se penche à son oreille.
Elle s'agite un peu, la voilà qui s'éveille,
Elle voudrait parler, la voilà qui s'endort
Plus pâle . . .

The title of the last of the 'récits', 'Amoureuse du Diable', also indicates its obvious links with the others, but again the long, involved story is couched in language which is prosaic in the extreme, as in these lines describing the heroine's total submission to the man who has seduced her:

> Ayant réalisé son avoir (sept ou huit
> Millions en billets de mille qu'on liasse
> Ne pèsent pas beaucoup et tiennent peu de place),
> Elle avait tassé tout dans un coffret mignon
> Et, le jour du départ, lorsque son compagnon,
> Dont du rhum bu de trop rendait la voix plus tendre,
> L'interrogea sur ce colis qu'il voyait pendre
> A son bras qui se lasse, elle répondit: 'Ça,
> C'est notre bourse' . . .

All too many of the remaining poems of *Jadis et Naguère* are of this kind—discursive, descriptive pieces, going into far too much detail and totally lacking in any emotional impact. It is perhaps unfair, or at least unkind, to cite a poem written as long before as 1869, but nevertheless 'La Soupe du Soir' does contain stanzas which epitomise the level to which *Jadis et Naguère* can so frequently sink and is typical of the early poems in the volume collectively sub-titled *Vers jeunes*:

> Tous se sont attablés pour manger de la soupe
> Et du bœuf, et ce tas sordide forme un groupe
> Dont l'ombre à l'infini s'allonge tout autour
> De la chambre, la lampe étant sans abat-jour.
>
> Les enfants sont petits et pâles, mais robustes
> En dépit des maigreurs saillantes de leurs bustes
> Qui disent les hivers passés sans feu souvent
> Et les étés subis dans un air étouffant . . .

The boring triviality of these lines is equalled by those of *Paysage*, originally written as a pastiche of François Coppée's manner in 1874, but clearly like Verlaine's own style when his aim is not to convey a deeply felt emotion but merely to describe the superficial details of a scene or an event:

> Vers Saint-Denis c'est bête et sale la campagne.
> C'est pourtant là qu'un jour j'emmenai ma compagne.
> Nous étions de mauvaise humeur et querellions.

> Un plat soleil d'été tartinait ses rayons
> Sur la plaine séchée ainsi qu'une rôtie.
> C'était pas trop après le Siège: une partie
> Des 'maisons de campagne' était à terre encor,
> D'autres se relevaient comme on hisse un décor,
> Et des obus tout neufs encastrés aux pilastres
> Portaient écrit autour: Souvenir des Désastres.

Such poems are scarcely worthy of further consideration, but there is one last poem in *Jadis et Naguère* which cannot be ignored, again because of its content as much as, and even more than its form, namely 'Art poétique', also written in prison, though in April 1874, several months after the 'récits diaboliques', and also intended for the abandoned *Cellulairement*. Its opening line must be one of the most frequently quoted in the whole of French literature:

> De la musique avant toute chose,

a line in which Verlaine formulated, in a simple and memorable way what was to become one of the basic tenets of Symbolism. The next line is less applicable to Symbolism in general than it is to Verlaine in particular, but it does emphasise Verlaine's peculiar, though not exclusive liking for uneven rhythms and the two following lines give some indication as to why he so often chose to use lines with an odd rather than an even number of syllables:

> Et pour cela préfère l'Impair
> Plus vague et plus soluble dans l'air,
> Sans rien en lui qui pèse ou qui pose . . .

All the later recommendations in the poem have the same basic idea—to break away from the well-composed, solidly constructed, thoughtfully argued, nicely rounded, evenly balanced kind of verse. 'L'indécis' is to be preferred to 'le précis', 'la nuance' to 'la couleur'; wit and irony have no place in poetry, nor has eloquence; rhyme must play a less dominant rôle:

> Il faut aussi que tu n'ailles point
> Choisir tes mots sans quelque méprise:
> Rien de plus cher que la chanson grise
> Où l'Indécis au Précis se joint.

C'est des beaux yeux derrière des voiles,
C'est le grand jour tremblant de midi,
C'est, par un ciel d'automne attiédi,
Le bleu fouillis des claires étoiles!

Car nous voulons la Nuance encor,
Pas la Couleur, rien que la nuance!
Oh! la nuance seule fiance
Le rêve au rêve et la flûte au cor!

Fuis du plus loin la Pointe assassine,
L'Esprit cruel et le Rire impur,
Qui font pleurer les yeux de l'Azur,
Et tout cet ail de basse cuisine!

Prends l'éloquence et tords-lui son cou!
Tu feras bien, en train d'énergie,
De rendre un peu la Rime assagie.
Si l'on n'y veille, elle ira jusqu'où?

O qui dira les torts de la Rime?
Quel enfant sourd ou quel nègre fou
Nous a forgé ce bijou d'un sou
Qui sonne creux et faux sous la lime?

In short, poetry must conserve a certain freedom and an air of spontaneity if it is to deserve the name of poetry; otherwise it is mere literature:

De la musique encore et toujours!
Que ton vers soit la chose envolée
Qu'on sent qui fuit d'une âme en allée
Vers d'autres cieux à d'autres amours.

Que ton vers soit la bonne aventure
Eparse au vent crispé du matin
Qui va fleurant la menthe et le thym...
Et tout le reste est littérature.

It is interesting to note that in 'Art poétique' Verlaine practises what he preaches in that the poem is in 'vers impairs' of nine syllables, there is a certain casual quality to the phrasing— 'c'est des beaux yeux', for example, instead of 'ce sont de beaux yeux', and 'prends l'éloquence et tords-lui son cou', instead of 'tords-lui le cou'—and the rhymes are almost all weak rhymes such as 'chose' and 'pose', 'Impair' and 'l'air', 'point' and 'joint', 'voiles' and 'étoiles' etc., with no supporting consonant before the vowel.

But it is no less interesting and indeed ironic to note also that at the very time when Verlaine wrote 'Art poétique' he was already beginning to move away from the kind of poetry he advocates towards precisely the kind of poetry he spurns. What appears therefore to be a manifesto for the future is in fact an account of the past. The poems that put into practice the precepts of 'Art poétique' had already been written, particularly in 1872 and 1873, and by the time 'Art poétique' was published in *Jadis et Naguère* in 1884 Verlaine had long ago abandoned its recommendations and was engaged in producing not poetry, but literature.

Amour

Although *Amour*, published in 1888, was originally intended as a sequel or companion volume to *Sagesse* (the 'amour' of the title being 'l'amour sacré', not 'l'amour profane') the religious poems in it are in fact very much in the minority, one-third of the volume being made up of a sequence of twenty-four poems in memory of Lucien Létinois, who had died five years before, and another third consisting of poems, sonnets for the most part, addressed to various friends, which would have been much better placed in the later volume *Dédicaces* and indeed half a dozen of them were repeated in that volume.

Jadis et Naguère did at least contain four or five poems of considerable interest as regards Verlaine's religious and literary ideas and of considerable merit as regards their poetic quality. The same cannot, unfortunately, be said of *Amour* which is a uniformly dull volume of verse, all too full of the long discursive kind of poem that Verlaine seemed increasingly able to turn out at will. Even one written as long before as 1875, 'J'ai naguère habité le meilleur des châteaux' cannot be excluded from this category and it was presumably for this reason that, after including it in the first manuscript of *Sagesse*, Verlaine dropped it from the final version and rejected it too for *Jadis et Naguère*. The first eight lines suffice to give something of the flavour, or insipidness, of this lengthy account, in ponderous alexandrines, of his life in the prison at Mons, the reader being spared no detail of its architecture, the materials used in its construction and even the colour of the paintwork:

> J'ai naguère habité le meilleur des châteaux
> Dans le plus fin pays d'eau vive et de coteaux:
> Quatre tours s'élevaient sur le front d'autant d'ailes,
> Et j'ai longtemps, longtemps habité l'une d'elles.
> Le mur, étant de brique extérieurement,
> Luisait rouge au soleil de ce site dormant,
> Mais un lait de chaux, clair comme une aube qui pleure
> Tendait légèrement la voûte intérieure . . .

The few religious poems are no better and again the opening lines of one of them, 'Un Conte', with their banal comparisons and sickly sentimentality offer a fair sample of the kind of thing which Verlaine was prepared to publish at this stage in his career:

> Simplement, comme on verse un parfum sur une flamme
> Et comme un soldat répand son sang pour la patrie,
> Je voudrais pouvoir mettre mon cœur avec mon âme
> Dans un beau cantique à la sainte Vierge Marie.
>
> Mais je suis, hélas! un pauvre pécheur trop indigne,
> Ma voix hurlerait parmi le chœur des voix des justes:
> Ivre encor du vin amer de la terrestre vigne,
> Elle pourrait offenser des oreilles augustes.
>
> Il faut un cœur pur comme l'eau qui jaillit des roches,
> Il faut qu'un enfant vêtu de lin soit notre emblème,
> Qu'un agneau bêlant n'éveille en nous aucuns reproches,
> Que l'innocence nous ceigne un brûlant diadème . . .

These lines were written as early as 1874, shortly after the conversion, as the unusual 'impair' rhythm of thirteen syllables suggests, and were presumably excluded from *Sagesse* and *Jadis et Naguère* because of their inferior quality or because of their similarity to those of the poem 'Je ne veux plus aimer que ma mère Marie . . .'

The poems in the Létinois cycle, written only shortly before the publication of *Amour*, show no improvement, as is evidenced by these quatrains detailing Verlaine's farming exploits with Lucien:

> Notre essai de culture eut une triste fin,
> Mais il fit mon délice un long temps et ma joie:
> J'y voyais se développer ton être fin
> Dans ce bon travail qui bénit ceux qu'il emploie:
>
> J'y voyais ton profil fluet sur l'horizon
> Marcher comme à pas vifs derrière la charrue,
> Gourmandant les chevaux ainsi que de raison,
> Sans colère, et criant diah et criant hue;
>
> Je te voyais herser, rouler, faucher parfois,
> Consultant les anciens, inquiet d'un nuage,
> L'hiver à la batteuse ou liant dans nos bois;
> Je t'aidais, vite hors d'haleine et tout en nage . . .

Finally a single quatrain from a sonnet addressed to the composer Emmanuel Chabrier will serve to indicate the level of the occasional verse which forms a substantial part of this ostensibly religious volume of verse:

> Chez ma mère charmante et divinement bonne,
> Votre génie improvisait au piano,
> Et c'était tout autour comme un brûlant anneau
> De sympathie et d'aise aimable qui rayonne . . .

One could forgive such lines, just as one forgives 'Birds in the Night' and 'Child Wife' in *Romances sans Paroles* and 'Prince mort en soldat . . .' in *Sagesse* if, as in those two volumes, there were other poems in *Amour* of true Verlainian quality, but, as the vast majority of critics would agree, there is not a single memorable poem in the entire volume. It is, however, only fair to mention that one critic, M. Antoine Adam, does not share this view. On the contrary, he perceives in the descriptive poems of *Amour*, and particularly in the Létinois cycle, signs of real poetic merit. He is especially impressed by the poem 'Bournemouth' and quotes the following verse to illustrate his point:

> Il fait un de ces temps ainsi que je les aime,
> Ni brume ni soleil! le soleil deviné,
> Pressenti, du brouillard mourant dansant à même
> Le ciel très haut qui tourne et fuit, rose de crême;
> L'atmosphère est de perle et la mer d'or fané . . .

But are these monotonously regular alexandrines with their leisurely sentence structure really in the same class as, for ex-

ample, 'L'Heure du Berger' from *Poèmes saturniens* which is on
a very similar subject?:

> La lune est rouge au brumeux horizon;
> Dans un brouillard qui danse la prairie
> S'endort fumeuse, et la grenouille crie
> Par les joncs verts où circule un frisson . . .

And it is important to bear in mind that whereas 'L'Heure du
Berger' is a poem of a mere twelve lines in three stanzas depicting the coming of night in a few swift and simple strokes,
'Bournemouth' trails on for sixty lines in twelve stanzas of which
M. Adam has chosen the one which, superficially, seems most
typical of Verlaine with its mist and twilight and muted colours.
Had he chosen the stanza which precedes it, or the one which
follows it, the way in which Verlaine goes into an excess of
prosaic detail enveloped in an unvarying rhythm would have
been much more obvious:

> A gauche la tour lourde (elle attend une flèche)
> Se dresse d'une église invisible d'ici;
> L'estacade très loin; haute, la tour, et sèche:
> C'est bien l'anglicanisme impérieux et rêche
> A qui l'essor du cœur vers le ciel manque aussi . . .
>
> De la tour protestante il part un chant de cloche,
> Puis deux et trois et quatre, et puis huit à la fois,
> Instinctive harmonie allant de proche en proche,
> Enthousiasme, joie, appel, douleur, reproche,
> Avec de l'or, du bronze et du feu dans la voix . . .

It is important to bear in mind too that 'Bournemouth' tells a
story and is in fact a piece of religious propaganda with Verlaine
being tempted by the Anglican church on his left, perhaps sym-
bolically, but being saved by the bells ringing out from the
Catholic church on his right:

> Ainsi Dieu parle par la voix de *sa* chapelle
> Sise à mi-côte à droite et sur le bord du bois . . .
> O Rome, ô Mère! Cri, geste qui nous rappelle
> Sans cesse au bonheur seul et donne au cœur rebelle
> Et triste le conseil pratique de la Croix.

Finally it is perhaps significant that this poem had been composed as long ago as 1877 and yet had not been included by

Verlaine in either *Sagesse* or *Jadis et Naguère*. It does therefore seem possible that the poet himself may not have agreed with M. Adam's opinion that in 'Bournemouth' 'ce qui domine, c'est l'humble adoration de la beauté' and that 'la beauté des *Paysages belges* est peut-être ici dépassée'.[3] As for M. Adam's similar defence of what he calls the 'Lamento pour Lucien Létinois', as Verlaine once described it in a letter to his friend Cazals, one example from this cycle has already been quoted, but another might be added as further proof of the wearisome detail into which Verlaine goes:

> O ses lettres d'alors! les miennes elles-mêmes!
> Je ne crois pas qu'il soit des choses plus suprêmes.
> J'étais, je ne puis dire mieux, vraiment très bien,
> Ou plutôt, je puis dire tout, vraiment chrétien.
> Je mettais tout mon soin pieux, toute l'étude
> Dont tout mon être était capable, à confirmer
> Cette âme dans l'effort de prier et d'aimer.

It may seem surprising that Verlaine should have written in these platitudinous terms, because one might have thought that Lucien Létinois could have re-kindled in him feelings not unlike those Rimbaud had inspired half a dozen years before. If this was the case, these feelings certainly never found adequate poetic expression, but it seems much more probable that, although attracted to Létinois, Verlaine was never carried away to the extent he was with Rimbaud. This is in fact made fairly clear in the fifteenth poem of the cycle:

> Je connus cet enfant, mon amère douceur,
> Dans un pieux collège où j'étais professeur.
> Ses dix-sept ans mutins et maigres, sa réelle
> Intelligence, et la pureté vraiment belle
> Que disaient et ses yeux et son geste et sa voix,
> Captivèrent mon cœur et dictèrent mon choix
> De lui pour fils, puisque, mon vrai fils, mes entrailles,
> On me le cache en manière de représailles
> Pour je ne sais quels torts charnels et surtout pour
> Un fier départ à la recherche de l'amour
> Loin d'une vie aux platitudes résignée . . .

Despite Verlaine's claims, it is difficult to see how the seventeen-year-old Létinois could have served as a substitute for his son

Georges Verlaine who, in 1877, was a mere six years old, but on the other hand it is all too easy to see how he could have served as a substitute for Rimbaud who had also been just seventeen when Verlaine had first met him towards the end of 1871. But the last few lines suggest that the memory of the Rimbaud episode was still vivid in Verlaine's mind and that Lucien was no more than a pale reflection of the 'époux infernal' with whom he had undertaken his 'fier départ à la recherche de l'amour'.

Parallèlement

It is interesting in this connection to note that, in Verlaine's next volume of verse, published in 1889, *Parallèlement*, the poem 'Laeti et Errabundi' is a frank and vividly clear recollection of the relationship with Rimbaud fifteen years before:

> Tout ce passé brûlant encore
> Dans mes veines et ma cervelle . . .

The meaning of the title is 'The Joyful Vagabonds' and the poem ends with Verlaine refusing to accept (quite correctly as it so happened) that the news he had heard of Rimbaud's death could possibly be true:

> Mort, tout ce triomphe inouï
> Retentissant sans frein ni fin
> Sur l'air jamais évanoui
> Que bat mon cœur qui fut divin!
>
> Quoi, le miraculeux poème
> Et la toute-philosophie,
> Et ma patrie et ma bohème
> Morts? Allons donc! tu vis ma vie.

In another poem too, without actually naming Rimbaud, Verlaine sings the praises of homosexual love with a fervour that goes far towards explaining how insipid later experiences must have seemed beside the memory of the years 1872 and 1873:

> Ces passions qu'eux seuls nomment encore amours
> Sont des amours aussi, tendres et furieuses,
> Avec des particularités curieuses
> Que n'ont pas les amours certes de tous les jours . . .

> La plénitude! Ils l'ont superlativement:
> Baisers repus, gorgés, mains privilégiées
> Dans la richesse des caresses repayées,
> Et ce divin final anéantissement!...
>
> Et ces réveils francs, clairs, riants, vers l'aventure
> De fiers damnés d'un plus magnifique sabbat!
> Et salut, témoins purs de l'âme en ce combat
> Pour l'affranchissement de la lourde nature!

But apart from these two recollections of Rimbaud there is only one other poem in *Parallèlement* which stands far above the general level, 'Impression fausse' written in prison in 1873 and originally intended for *Cellulairement*. Here, for almost the first time since *Sagesse*, the true Verlainian note can once more be detected in the muted colours of these short 'vers impairs' with their touching simplicity of syntax and vocabulary:

> Dame souris trotte,
> Noire dans le gris du soir,
> Dame souris trotte,
> Grise dans le noir.
>
> On sonne la cloche:
> Dormez, les bons prisonniers,
> On sonne la cloche:
> Faut que vous dormiez...
>
> Dame souris trotte,
> Rose dans les rayons bleus.
> Dame souris trotte:
> Debout, paresseux!

The remaining half-dozen poems taken from *Cellulairement* are not of the same quality, and it is indeed instructive to compare with 'Impression fausse' another poem written at about the same time and originally entitled 'Promenade au Préau'. At first sight the latter appears to be a very similar sort of poem with a mixture of short lines of two different lengths having as its subject prisoners walking round and round as their daily exercise. But instead of the uncertain 'impair' rhythm of five and seven syllables arranged in an uneven pattern of 5, 7, 5, 5, these are firmer lines of eight and four syllables arranged in a balanced pattern of 8, 4, 4, 4, 8, 4, 4, 4. It seems unlikely that Verlaine intended this regular pattern to suggest the prisoners circling round, since the change in rhythm destroys this effect, in contrast, for example, with the extreme regularity of 'Tournez, tournez, bons chevaux de bois' in *Romances sans Paroles* and *Sagesse*. As far as other features are concerned, the simple, repetitive vocabulary and straightforward syntax of 'Impression fausse' give way to a more extensive and unusual vocabulary and a relatively involved sentence structure. The poem begins somewhat unhappily with an excruciating pun on 'souci' in its two senses of 'marigold' and 'care', the second stanza has a rather 'recherché' metaphor equating the prisoners circling round with Samson turning the millwheel at Gaza, and in the fourth stanza, after yet another metaphor, comparing the prisoners with a circus, Verlaine begins to analyse and comment on his situation:

> La cour se fleurit de souci
>   Comme le front
>   De tous ceux-ci
>   Qui vont en rond
> En flageolant sur leur fémur
>   Débilité
>   Le long du mur
>   Fou de clarté.
>
> Tournez, Samsons sans Dalila,
>   Sans Philistin,
>   Tournez bien la
>   Meule au destin.
> Vaincu risible de la loi,
>   Mouds tour à tour
>   Ton cœur, ta foi
>   Et ton amour ! . . .
>
> J'en suis de ce cirque effaré,
>   Soumis d'ailleurs
>   Et préparé
>   A tous le malheurs.
> Et pourquoi si j'ai contristé
>   Ton vœu têtu,
>   Société,
>   Me choierais-tu ? . . .

The remaining poems taken from *Cellulairement* have the same dull, flat, prosaic tone as Verlaine describes the sounds he can hear from his cell:

L'aile où je suis donnant juste sur une gare,
J'entends de nuit (mes nuits sont blanches) la bagarre
Des machines qu'on chauffe et des trains ajustés . . .

or complains that he is being ostracised by the literary world:

Las! je suis à l'Index et dans les dédicaces
Me voici Paul V . . . pur et simple. Les audaces
De mes amis, tant les éditeurs sont des saints.
Doivent éliminer mon nom de leurs desseins . . .

As for the rest of *Parallèlement* it is largely the same kind of ragbag as *Jadis et Naguère*. It opens with half a dozen Lesbian poems under the general sub-title *Les Amies*, that Verlaine had already published clandestinely over twenty years before in 1868 under the pseudonym of Pablo de Herlagnez, and these set the tone for the volume as a whole which, ostensibly, is a collection of sensual poetry parallel to the ostensibly religious poetry of *Amour*. But just as *Amour* soon drifts, after the first few pages, into decidedly secular verse, so *Parallèlement*, after a further half dozen poems of recent composition under the general sub-title *Filles*, drifts into the poems from *Cellulairement* mentioned above, which have nothing whatever to do with the sins of the flesh, and ends with a couple of dozen poems on a variety of subjects that were clearly added simply to bring the volume up to an acceptable size rather than to pursue the theme of profane love parallel to the sacred love of the previous volume.

V

THE LAST POEMS

Dédicaces, Bonheur, Chansons pour Elle, Liturgies intimes, Odes en son honneur, Elégies, Dans les Limbes, Épigrammes, Chair, Invectives, Œuvres posthumes

Edmond Lepelletier, in his study of Verlaine published in 1907, was among the first to state categorically that after 1889 Verlaine's talent 'fit naufrage',[1] and the vast majority of critics since then have accepted this view. In 1924 Pierre Martino cautiously agreed that 'il est bien difficile, à moins d'être un admirateur fétichiste ou de se plaire surtout à des curiosités anecdotiques, de ne pas avouer que l'intérêt des dernières œuvres, dans leur ensemble, est assez médiocre'.[2] In 1948 Y. G. Le Dantec wrote, with regard to *Dédicaces*: 'Avec ce volume commence la dernière époque, l'irrémédiable déclin . . . une fois vidés de la matière qui avait servi a former *Parallèlement*, les tiroirs de Pauvre Lélian ne contenaient plus rien et il était alors, et pour jamais, incapable de les remplir à nouveau'.[3]

In 1953 however, Antoine Adam, if not an 'admirateur fétichiste', was at least determined to insist, though not, unfortunately, to demonstrate, that Verlaine's poetic talent did not totally collapse in the last ten years of his life. He praises the 'variété de ton' and the 'souplesse de talent' of *Dédicaces*, the 'sérénité, largeur nouvelle de vues, lucidité d'un esprit apaisé et purifié' of 'le charmant volume d'*Epigrammes*', and 'des pièces excellentes de verve ou superbes d'indignation' which he finds in *Invectives*.[4] As for the religious volumes, he severely criticises *Bonheur* but nevertheless detects in it a sufficient number of good poems to allow him to conclude that it is 'dans l'ensemble un grand livre' and he judges *Liturgies intimes* even more harshly but again considers that the volume contains 'de fort belles pièces'.[5] In the case of the volumes written 'in parallel', he dismisses the poems in *Chansons pour Elle* as being on the whole 'déplaisants et ridicules' but excuses them on the grounds that they are after all 'chansons' and that Verlaine was trying to imitate the rhythms of popular songs; on the other hand *Odes en son Honneur* needs no such excuse since M. Adam finds these poems markedly superior to the *Chansons pour Elle* and considers that they herald a revival of Verlaine's talent in his last years that is continued, in M. Adam's view, if not in *Chair* and *Dans les Limbes*, to which he awards neither praise nor blame, at least in the 'authentique et triste beauté' of the *Elégies*.[6]

M. Adam did not, however, succeed in winning the critics over to his side. In 1960 Jacques Borel dismissed *Dédicaces* as 'politesses aux uns et aux autres, vagues confrères, directeurs de revue, journalistes, hommages à quelques poètes authentiques' and he added that 'Verlaine semble avoir définitivement perdu dans *Dédicaces* le secret de son propre chant'.[7] As for *Epigrammes*, he pointed out that Verlaine himself apologetically wrote the following preface to the volume: 'L'opuscule que voici fut écrit par un malade qui voulait se distraire et ne pas trop ennuyer ses contemporains. En conséquence la postérité est priée de n'y voir qu'un jeu'. The third of the volumes of occasional verse, *Invectives*, M. Borel describes in the following terms: 'Haines, rancunes, vase remuée, dépits attisés, la fureur du poète s'étend ici à toute chose'.[8] His criticism of the religious volumes, *Bonheur* and *Liturgies intimes*, is equally severe: 'Tous les thèmes anciens, mais vidés soudain de leur substance ... non plus chantés, mais récités, expliqués ...'[9] With regard to *Chansons pour Elle* M. Borel is prepared to agree with M. Adam that they may have been intended by Verlaine as 'chansons de café-concert', but he nevertheless finds the volume 'poétiquement démunie ... paillardises laborieuses, chansons gauloises, anecdotes grotesques ou sordides ... la faiblesse du jeu poétique accentue la boiterie de l'œuvre ...'[10] In the second of the two volumes devoted to 'l'amour profane', *Odes en son Honneur*, M. Borel entirely fails to detect the 'adorable fraîcheur de jadis', the 'vibration', the 'élan'[11] that M. Adam had discerned; on the contrary he considers that 'l'amour pour la chair usée, la pitié ou la tendresse pour la vieille "amazone" dégradée ... ne passent pas du plan de la réalité décrite, indentifiable, à celui de la vérité poétique'. 'Le secret de l'âme', he concludes, 'n'affleure plus sous un art impuissant désormais à la sensation et à la suggestion'.[12] Since M. Borel does not agree with M. Adam that there is a revival of

Verlaine's talent in *Odes en son Honneur* he inevitably disagrees with him too about the continuation of any such revival in *Elégies* in which he sees not 'une authentique et triste beauté' but 'la vulgarité, le prosaïsme constamment'.[13]

More recent critics have confirmed M. Borel's refusal to allow M. Adam's defence of Verlaine's final volumes to alter the generally accepted view that they contain little or nothing of any merit. A. E. Carter, writing in 1969, describes *Dédicaces, Epigrammes* and *Invectives* as 'bits and pieces written by a man who could always turn a stanza and turned far too many'. *Bonheur* he finds 'a dreary affair' in which 'the dogmatism from which even *Sagesse* is not entirely free now stifles all genuine religious sentiment', while *Liturgies intimes* he dismisses as having 'even less interest'. The parallel volumes, *Chansons pour Elle, Odes en son Honneur, Elégies* and *Dans les Limbes* are judged with the same kind of severity: 'It is mostly poor stuff, and even the technical eccentricities—the slang, the daring half-rhymes, the dislocated prosody—do not suffice to keep one reading'.[14]

Miss Joanna Richardson, writing in 1971, concurs with these views. She suggests, like Lepelletier, that by 1890 Verlaine had become what she calls 'poetically impotent' and that from then on he was writing simply from habit or from financial need.[15] Just as M. Borel drew attention to Verlaine's apologetic preface to *Epigrammes*, so she draws attention to the final lines of a poem Verlaine addressed to the young English advocate of Symbolism, Arthur Symons, in 1894 where he looks back sadly and nostalgically to the days of *Fêtes galantes* and recognises that now he is no more than a ruin of his former self:

> 'Et le jet d'eau ride l'humble bassin',
> Comme chantait, quand il avait votre âge,
> L'auteur de ces vers-ci, débris d'orage
> Ruine, épave, au vague et lent dessein.[16]

Miss Richardson goes on to criticise Verlaine's last volumes individually; in *Dédicaces* she finds that 'the poems to his mistresses lack conviction and quality, the poems to his friends and acquaintances impress only by their mediocrity';[17] *Epigrammes* she dismisses as 'superficial, a medley of poems with no consistent theme and no fire';[18] *Bonheur* she classes as 'a religious book written without conviction, a series of poems which seem more like literary exercises than a record of belief'.[19] The inspiration of *Liturgies intimes* she finds 'sadly wanting'.[20] She castigates *Chansons pour Elle* for 'the banality of the language and of certain rhythms, the facility or vulgarity of many of the themes' and quotes from a review in the *Mercure de France* where a contemporary critic defined the volume as 'doggerel by a poet of genius'.[21] In *Odes en son Honneur*, where M. Adam found so much to commend, she sees only 'a repetitive catalogue of his mistress's charms, a description of everyday incidents in their life; the poems have no depth, no general significance' and *Elégies* appears to her no more than 'a prosaic record of a turbulent and common liaison'.[22]

The balance of critical opinion has therefore remained very heavily weighted against M. Adam, and when one examines in some detail one of the few poems M. Adam actually specifies as being among those which he finds of first-rate quality one cannot but be convinced that his judgement is suspect. It is presumably the following poem from *Bonheur* that M. Adam has in mind when he praises Verlaine for his evocation of 'la mélancolie des soirs de Toussaint':[23]

> Immédiatement après le salut somptueux,
> Le luminaire éteint, moins les seuls cierges liturgiques
> Les psaumes pour les morts sont dits sur un mode mineur
> Par les clercs et le peuple saisi de mélancolie.
>
> Un glas lent se répand des clochers de la cathédrale
> Répandu par tous les campaniles du diocèse,
> Et plane et pleure sur les villes et sur la campagne
> Dans la nuit tôt venue en la saison arriérée.
>
> Chacun s'en fut coucher reconduit par la voix dolente
> Et douce à l'infini de l'airain commémoratoire
> Qui va bercer le sommeil un peu triste des vivants
> Du souvenir des décédés de toutes les paroisses.

This poem undoubtedly has unusual features which at first glance tempt one, and no doubt tempted M. Adam, to class it as typically Verlainian in that it has fourteen syllables to the line and has no true rhymes but merely assonance throughout. In fact, however neither of these two features is to be found in any of the poems Verlaine published when he was at the height of his powers and one wonders therefore whether the desire to break free from conventional forms has now become itself a convention and whether Verlaine is consciously and even self-consciously trying to be original. In the earlier volumes one never felt that Verlaine was pursuing originality for its own sake, but here there seems no justification for the fourteen-syllable line, or for the absence of rhyme. In 'Soleils couchants' the unusual 'impair' rhythm arose naturally from the words and the phrasing:

> Une aube affaiblie
> Verse par les champs
> La mélancolie
> Des soleils couchants . . .

as did the absence of a rhyme for the second line in:

> Il pleure dans mon cœur
> Comme il pleut sur la ville,
> Quelle est cette langueur
> Qui pénètre mon cœur . . .

But in the poem from *Bonheur* one feels on the contrary that Verlaine has had to force the words into an artificial framework. An adverb such as 'immédiatement' smacks of being a piece of padding, as does the adjective 'liturgique' associated with 'cierge' since the latter is, by definition, connected with church ritual. The obvious rhyme for 'liturgiques' would be 'mélancoliques', but Verlaine studiously avoids it with the paraphrase 'saisi de mélancolie'. So as to provide extra syllables in the line an awkward synonym for 'clochers' has to be used, 'campaniles'. The usual expression 'arrière-saison' is clumsily and not altogether accurately replaced by 'saison arriérée'. The sad sound of the bells tolling on All Saints Day becomes, in a painful periphrasis, 'la voix dolente de l'airain commémoratoire'.

Associated with this artificiality the poem has the long-standing Verlaine weakness of going into far too much detail in the most prosaic way—the scene described takes place not just 'après le salut somptueux' but 'immédiatement après'; the psalms are not merely sung, but sung in a minor key, and not simply by the priests, but by the people too; not only does the bell toll from the cathedral, or more specifically, from the cathedral towers, but also from all the other bell towers in the diocese, and not only over the town but over the countryside as well; and the bells toll not just in memory of the dead, or even of the dead of the parishes, but of the dead of all the parishes. Such painstaking detail is reminiscent of the tedious descriptive verse of *La Bonne Chanson* or the political poems of *Sagesse*, and, as in those poems, there is none of the hesitancy and air of spontaneity that characterises Verlaine's best poetry. On the contrary, the rhythm, though unusual, is regular to the point of being ponderous and the syntax is carefully ordered. In fact, if the poem were not set out in stanza form it could easily be read as a passage of prose since there is nothing in it to lift it into the realm of poetry.

'Agnus Dei' is another poem, this time from *Liturgies intimes*, in which M. Adam considers that Verlaine has avoided his 'vieux penchant vers le didactisme' and has instead 'laissé affluer des images chargées de signification'.[24] Again this is a poem which, superficially, looks typically Verlainian in that it is made up of tercets each of nine-, eleven- and thirteen-syllable lines. But in fact this too is a pattern of 'vers impairs' that Verlaine had never used in his early volumes and there is something strangely stilted and artificial about an arrangement whereby every line in each verse is of a different length:

> L'agneau cherche l'amère bruyère,
> C'est le sel et non le sucre qu'il préfère,
> Son pas fait le bruit d'une averse sur la poussière.
>
> Quand il veut un but, rien ne l'arrête,
> Brusque, il fonce avec de grands coups de sa tête,
> Puis il bêle vers sa mère accourue inquiète . . .
>
> Agneau de Dieu, qui sauves les hommes,
> Agneau de Dieu, qui nous comptes et nous nommes,
> Agneau de Dieu, vois, prends pitié de ce que nous sommes.
>
> Donne-nous la paix et non la guerre,
> O l'agneau terrible en ta juste colère,
> O toi, seul Agneau, Dieu le seul fils de Dieu le Père.

As for the imagery, it is difficult to share M. Adam's appreciation on this point. The second line has a faintly ludicrous touch to it, even if one assumes that the lamb's preference for salt rather than sugar symbolises Christ's desire to save the sinners rather than the virtuous. The image in the third line, however, seems quite pointless and has, one suspects, been introduced by Verlaine in order to bring in 'poussière' as a rhyme for 'bruyère' and 'préfère'. The second stanza may well be an accurate account of a real lamb's activities, but it is difficult to see how this picture can symbolise satisfactorily the activities of the lamb of God of the title, particularly the third line, unless its meaning is that Christ appeals for help to the Virgin Mary who comes to his aid. If this is the case, then it is surely an unfortunate image, reminiscent of those lines in *Romances sans Paroles* where Verlaine had complained to Mathilde that

> . . . vous bêlâtes vers votre mère—ô douleur—
> Comme un triste agnelet . . .

The third stanza moves from the symbol of the lamb to the figure of Christ himself, and here one has very much the feeling that the third line, instead of reading 'Agneau de Dieu, prends pitié de nous', has been arbitrarily and clumsily extended so as to cover thirteen syllables and so as to provide a rhyme for 'hommes' and 'nommes'. Similarly, in the final stanza one feels that there is little justification for the introduction of the words 'guerre' and 'colère', other than to provide rhymes for 'Dieu le Père', and that the word 'seul' is used not just once but twice in the last line for the sole purpose of providing two extra syllables.

Although this kind of criticism can be made of almost every line in Verlaine's last volumes of verse, M. Adam is not quite the only critic to have tried to salvage something from the wreckage. L. Morice defends[25] the trilogy of religious poems first published in 1894, 'Tristia', 'Meliora' and 'Optima', which, like the poems that have just been quoted, seem at first glance to be typically Verlainian in that two of them are in octosyllabic tercets, with each tercet having a single rhyme, while the third one is in twelve-syllable rhyming couplets. On closer inspection, however, they too prove to have that element of padding and that clumsiness of construction that is so conspicuously absent from Verlaine's free-flowing earlier poems:

> Je n'avais pas connu l'Ennui,
> Pourtant jusqu'au jour d'aujourd'hui
> Je vivais et mourais de lui.

> Ce depuis l'atroce journée,
> Où, pauvre âme au ciel ramenée,
> J'ai méconnu ma destinée.
>
> Ramenée au ciel, et comment?
> Par le fait logique et charmant
> D'un grand miracle assurément,
>
> Par la conversion soudaine
> D'un cœur voué tout à la haine
> En un d'une onction sereine . . .

These opening lines from 'Tristia', weighed down by such super-
fluities as 'jusqu'au jour d'aujourd'hui' and the adverb 'assurément', by the monotonously regular rhythm, by the awkwardly
inserted 'ce' and by the cacophony of 'en un d'une onction
sereine' seem utterly different from those of 'En bateau' in *Fêtes
galantes*, though in fact the latter poem is also written in octosyllabic tercets each of which has a single rhyme:

> L'étoile du berger tremblote
> Dans l'eau plus noire, et le pilote
> Cherche un briquet dans sa culotte.
>
> C'est l'instant, Messieurs, ou jamais,
> D'être audacieux, et je mets
> Mes deux mains partout désormais . . .
>
> Cependant la lune se lève
> Et l'esquif en sa course brève
> File gaîment sur l'eau qui rêve.

'Optima' too seems to have a quite different rhythm from 'En
Bateau', again because of the extreme regularity of the lines
which is made worse by the catalogue effect of Verlaine listing
his good intentions as he had done in *La Bonne Chanson*:

> La simplicité dans la vérité;
> La sincérité dans l'humilité;
> L'humble austérité dans l'obscurité;
>
> L'obscurité dans le simple devoir;
> Le tort d'autrui, prier, ne pas le voir;
> Le sien propre, prier pour le savoir;
>
> En tout donner l'exemple si l'on peut;
> En rien ne pas faire ce que l'on veut,
> Qu'aimer Dieu d'un cœur qui veut et qui peut.

The third poem of the trilogy, 'Meliora' can be compared and contrasted with the opening poem of *Sagesse*, 'Bon chevalier masqué' (see p. 58 above), which follows the same pattern of twelve-syllable rhyming couplets. But whereas the latter is made up of a mere ten couplets in which the allegory of the masked horseman thrusting a lance through the poet's heart and then giving him new life is quickly and captivatingly told, 'Meliora' consists of sixteen couplets forming what L. Morice calls, in an unintentionally critical phrase, 'un long soupir vers le bonheur'. Its repetitions are not the casual, irregular recurrence of certain words in different contexts as in 'Bon chevalier masqué . . .', but a monotonous insistence on the same point:

> Dix ans de vice ancien et de vieille sottise
> Revenus à la piste en une tête grise,
>
> Dix ans, Seigneur en Croix! d'un âge mûrissant
> Menant son train honteux d'impur adolescent . . .

The simple emotional effects of the earlier poem are replaced by a complex, hair-splitting self-analysis:

> O la foi d'un enfant par soi refait jadis!
> Perdue? ô non, mon Dieu, dans ces dix ans maudits,
>
> Offensée, et c'est trop, c'est affreux, mais perdue,
> O non, mon Dieu d'amour, et toute l'amour due,
>
> Tout le respect, malgré l'offense de la chair,
> Point de l'âme, aveuglée en ces lueurs d'enfer,
>
> Le regret rédempteur, le remords qui délivre,
> Ah! du bon est resté dans ce cœur naguère ivre,
>
> Dans cet esprit qui fut détourné, rien de plus,
> Ah! du bon a veillé dans ce sommeil perclus . . .

The defects of the religious poems in Verlaine's last volumes of verse are repeated in the secular poems that he wrote in parallel, and although it would clearly be a long and unrewarding task to prove the point beyond all possible doubt, the general level of achievement of his occasional verse and of the poems addressed to his mistresses may be fairly indicated by the following lines chosen from *Dédicaces*, *Odes en son Honneur* and *Elégies* respectively:

> Je n'ai vu Manchester que d'un coin de Salford,
> Donc très mal et très peu, quel que fût mon effort

A travers le brouillard et les courses pénibles
Au possible, en dépit d'hansoms inaccessibles
Presque, grâce à ma jambe male et mes pieds bots . . .

*   *   *

Nos repas sont charmants encore que modestes,
Grâce à ton art profond d'accommoder les restes
Du rôti d'hier ou de ce récent pot-au-feu
En hâchis et ragoûts comme on n'en trouve pas chez Dieu . . .

*   *   *

D'après ce que j'ai vu, d'après ce que je sais,
D'après ce que je crois, nuls n'ont plus de succès,
Ou n'en eurent, ou n'en auront, si c'est ma veine,
Auprès de toi, sinon ceux simples et sans gêne:
Tel un moi qui serait plus jeune, au moins de corps,
Quoique je ne me mets pas au rang des morts
Encore ou bien déjà, n'en déplaise aux quarante
Et trop d'ans qui sont, las! ma seule sûre rente . . .

If these are the kind of poems M. Adam has in mind when he talks of Verlaine's 'souplesse de talent' in *Dédicaces*, the 'adorable fraîcheur de jadis' of *Odes en son Honneur* and the 'authentique et triste beauté' of *Elégies*, it is scarcely surprising that other critics have refused to be won over to his side and that they have continued to condemn as severely as earlier critics the vast quantities of verse that Verlaine turned out in the last half dozen years of his life.

There is, moreover, a perfectly reasonable explanation as to why this shipwreck of Verlaine's talent should have occurred. As has been shown, and as critics such as Octave Nadal and Jacques Borel in particular have emphasised, Verlaine was a poet who achieved the best results when subject to powerful emotional impulses. Such impulses were provided by the adolescent longings in *Poèmes saturniens*, the youthful curiosities and disappointments in *Fêtes galantes*, the initial stages of the love affair with Mathilde in *La Bonne Chanson*, the irresistible fascination of Rimbaud's personality in *Romances sans Paroles*, and the grief at his arrest and imprisonment, followed by the ardour of his conversion, in the early poems of *Sagesse*. But once Verlaine had run the whole gamut of human emotions in this way, it is not surprising that he should have been incapable of being deeply moved by any further experiences later in life. It seems certain, as has been mentioned (see p. 86 above), that Lucien Létinois was no more than a pale reflection of Rimbaud. In similar fashion Verlaine's religion of his later years was no more than a lifeless imitation of his fervent Christianity of 1874 and 1875 and his affairs with Eugénie Krantz and Philomène Boudin no more than faint echoes of the ecstatic happiness of 'La lune blanche . . .' and 'Avant que tu ne t'en ailles . . .' Lacking any emotional impulse to write, but driven to do so by the necessity to earn a living, Verlaine, from 1880 onwards, simply used up old poems that he had left unpublished and then, increasingly as these reserves were depleted, proceeded to refurbish his old themes, lapsing permanently into that wordy, descriptive, prosaic kind of style that, throughout his career as a poet, he had, at times, tended to adopt.

VI

THE PROSE WORKS

Although Verlaine is known primarily as a poet, he wrote a considerable amount of prose which in fact forms about one-quarter of his total output, excluding his voluminous correspondence. These prose works can be broadly divided into three kinds, literary criticism, works of fiction and memoirs, all three of which Verlaine toyed with at various times throughout his career, although the memoirs naturally tend to be concentrated in the last years of his life.

Literary criticism

Verlaine's very first publication was a piece of literary criticism in the magazine *L'Art* in November and December 1865. It was, moreover, criticism of a critic in that it was a lengthy review of *Les Œuvres et les Hommes* by Jules Barbey d'Aurevilly, the contemporary of Hugo and Musset who remained the powerful defender of the old Romantic aesthetic against the newer principles of the Parnassians. Verlaine makes this point at the very beginning of his article where he is scathing about 'la sympathie de l'auteur pour les inspirés' and his 'dédain superbe des travailleurs'. He describes this as 'un point de vue quinquagénaire' and attributes it to the fact that in his youth Barbey d'Aurevilly had been among the 'témoins enthousiastes des prouesses de l'inspiration' and is consequently 'tout ébahi en présence des œuvres de la nouvelle école qui a, comme on sait, ce ridicule de penser que les beaux vers ne se font pas tout seuls et que les rimes pauvres n'entraînent pas fatalement la richesse des images, ni même celle des idées'. These sarcastic comments demonstrate that at that date Verlaine clearly considered himself as belonging to the Parnassian movement and strongly echo the lines from the *Epilogue* of the *Poèmes saturniens* (see p. 12 above) where Verlaine also mocks inspiration and preaches the virtue of working at one's poems.[1]

But not only does this article reveal what Verlaine's aesthetic views were at the age of twenty-one, it also reveals a critical judgement which is surprisingly perceptive in one so young. The passage on Leconte de Lisle, for example, deserves to be quoted in full for its sober and sympathetic assessment of his *Poèmes antiques* and *Poèmes barbares*: 'Leconte de Lisle est une des victimes de M. Barbey d'Aurevilly, et, au fait, on devait s'y attendre. Que pouvait-il comprendre, lui, le passionné, à cette poésie calme, rassise, à ces vers d'airain retentissant comme des tonnerres lointains, sans jamais éclater, par cette suprême loi de l'art que tout éclat est une discordance, et que le beau, c'est l'harmonie. Et que pouvait comprendre ce catholique farouche . . . à ce vaste plan synthétique de l'œuvre du grand poète, où chaque religion vient à son tour fournir sa pierre à un monument sans analogue dans aucune littérature, et dont l'ensemble, large et profond, philosophiquement parlant, a, comme art, la sérénité de la Grèce, la force de Rome et la splendeur de l'Inde?'.

Similarly Verlaine springs to the defence of Flaubert's *Salammbô*, praising 'le style rhythmé, les descriptions éblouissantes, les batailles magnifiquement évoquées, les personnages épiques et, par-dessus tout, la fable si simple et si terrible' and pouring scorn on Barbey d'Aurevilly's opinion that '*Salammbô* est tombé définitivement dans le plus juste oubli . . . M. Flaubert m'a fait l'effet de n'avoir plus rien dans le ventre . . .' This last remark was of course to be amply disproved and Verlaine's confidence in Flaubert's genius amply vindicated by the publication of *L'Education sentimentale* four years later in 1869. Gautier too is defended against Barbey d'Aurevilly's attacks on *Le Capitaine Fracasse* as 'un morceau de tapisserie faite d'après les tableaux plus ou moins oubliés, ou empoussiérés maintenant, de ces maîtres qu'on appelle Scarron, Cyrano de Bergerac et, pour mieux dire, tous les romanciers du commencement du XVIIe siècle que M. Gautier a imités dans ce roman sans *vie* et sans *passion* réelle . . .' Again Verlaine mocks Barbey d'Aurevilly's Romantic insistence on 'passion' and urges him to admire instead 'la langue splendide de ce roman picaresque'.

Not only does Verlaine thus show himself to be a sounder critic than Barbey d'Aurevilly in his appreciation of these major figures, but posterity has also confirmed his refusal to accept the latter's exaggerated praise for two minor Romantics, Roger de

Beauvoir and Amédée Pommier. None would now dispute Verlaine's judgement that the former, though a 'nouvelliste agréable' is far from being a great poet and that the latter can most certainly not be put alongside Dante, as Barbey d'Aurevilly rashly claims.

This impression that the young Verlaine had a promising critical faculty is strengthened when one turns to the second article he published in *L'Art*, also in November and December 1865, on Baudelaire. This too deserves to be quoted at some length since Verlaine not only deals curtly with the facile and frequent jibes that were current at the time about Baudelaire being 'celui qui a chanté la charogne', he also defines the really fundamental importance of *Les Fleurs du Mal* with a sureness of touch that few, if any, more experienced professional critics of his day could equal:

La profonde originalité de Charles Baudelaire c'est, à mon sens, de représenter puissamment et essentiellement l'homme moderne... l'homme physique moderne, tel que l'ont fait les raffinements d'une civilisation excessive, l'homme moderne avec ses sens aiguisés et vibrants, son esprit douloureusement subtil... L'historien futur de notre époque devra, pour ne pas être incomplet, feuilleter attentivement et religieusement ce livre qui est la quintessence et comme la concentration extrême de tout un élément de ce siècle. Pour preuve de ce que j'avance, prenons, en premier lieu, les poèmes amoureux du volume des *Fleurs du Mal*. Comment l'auteur a-t-il exprimé ce sentiment de l'amour, le plus magnifique des lieux communs... En païen comme Goethe, en chrétien comme Pétrarque, ou, comme Musset, en enfant? En rien de tout cela, et c'est son immense mérite... L'amour, dans les vers de Charles Baudelaire, c'est bien l'amour d'un Parisien du XIXe siècle, quelque chose de fiévreux et d'analysé à la fois.

Verlaine's comments on Baudelaire's attitude to poetry are no less perceptive and he singles out what has since become an often quoted phrase: 'La poésie... n'a d'autre but qu'elle-même'. He also quotes with understanding and approval Baudelaire's attempt to define the subtle amalgam of emotional involvement and intellectual detachment that go to make up a poem and that many other poets, from Wordsworth to Valéry, have defined less satisfactorily perhaps than Baudelaire:

Le principe de la poésie est, strictement et simplement, l'aspiration humaine vers une beauté supérieure et la manifestation de ce principe est dans un enthousiasme, une excitation à l'âme—enthousiasme tout à fait indépendant de la passion qui est l'ivresse du cœur ... Car la passion est *naturelle*, trop naturelle pour ne pas introduire un ton blessant, discordant, dans le domaine de la Beauté pure ...[2]

As well as picking out this important issue Verlaine has his own comment to make on the matter when he points out that one of the striking features of Baudelaire's poetry is that one detects 'au milieu de l'expression du plus grand enthousiasme, de la plus vive douleur, etc., le sentiment d'un très grand calme ...'. Finally he has some pertinent comments to make on the technique of Baudelaire's poetry—his use of the 'rejet', his attenuation, in certain lines, of the caesura, and the splendid, sweeping balance of such lines as: 'J'ai plus de souvenirs que si j'avais mille ans'.

After such a promising beginning one might have hoped that Verlaine would have gone on to become a critic of some note, but, apart from half a dozen short articles and reviews in various magazines in 1867, it was not until almost twenty years later, in 1883, that he returned to literary criticism with three articles under the intriguing title of *Les Poètes maudits*, first published in the magazine *Lutèce* and then in volume form a few months later in 1884. These articles, on Tristan Corbière, Arthur Rimbaud and Stéphane Mallarmé met with considerable success and in 1885 Verlaine began a second series of three articles, first in *Lutèce* and then in another magazine, *La Vogue*. These three articles too, on Marceline Desbordes-Valmore, Villiers de l'Isle-Adam and Verlaine himself, under the anagrammatic pseudonym of Pauvre Lélian, were published in book form, along with the first three, in 1888.

The immediately obvious difference between these six articles and the two earlier ones on Barbey d'Aurevilly and Baudelaire is that the later ones are much less substantial. Verlaine himself, towards the end of the essay on Pauvre Lélian, deprecatingly describes *Les Poètes maudits* as 'un petit livre de critique—ô de critique! d'exaltation plutôt', and the articles are in fact largely made up of quotations from the poets concerned preceded by brief admiring comments. Even in the article on Rimbaud, Verlaine has extraordinarily little to say about a poet whom he must have known better than anyone else. It is true that, after giving the biographical background to 'Les Assis' he accurately describes it as an example of 'la puissance d'ironie et la verve terrible du poète' and that his judgement of 'Les Effarés' as 'farouche et tendre, caricatural et cordial' is as perceptive as his assessment of 'Les Chercheuses de Poux'—'le beau balancement lamartinien, n'est-ce pas, dans ces quelques vers qui semblent se prolonger dans du rêve et de la musique'. But 'Le Bateau ivre', though quoted in full, is accompanied by no comment of any kind, nor are the sonnets 'Voyelles' and 'Oraison du Soir'. And if Verlaine could find so little to say about the poetry of his one time 'compagnon d'enfer', it is not to be wondered at that he has even less to say about the work of Mallarmé, seven of whose poems are quoted in full, thus taking up considerably more than half the ten-page article, but are left without comment save for the occasional complimentary adjective such as 'l'exquise "Apparition" ', 'l'adorable "Sainte" ' and 'le beau "Tombeau d'Edgar Poe" '. The essay on Corbière is shorter still and again well over half the article is devoted to lengthy quotations accompanied by remarks which are clearly little more than mere padding, as in the following paragraph:

Comme rimeur et comme prosodiste il n'a rien d'impeccable, c'est-à-dire d'assommant. Nul d'entre les Grands comme lui n'est impeccable, à commencer par Homère qui somnole quelquefois, pour aboutir à Goethe le très humain, quoiqu'on die, en passant par le plus qu'irrégulier Shakespeare . . .

The same kind of rambling remarks characterise the opening essay in the second series:

Nous avons dit que la langue de Marceline Desbordes-Valmore était suffisante, c'est très suffisante qu'il fallait dire; seulement nous sommes d'un tel purisme, d'un tel pédantisme, ajouterons-nous, puisque l'on nous en appelle un décadent (injure, entre parenthèses, pittoresque, très automne, bien soleil couchant, à ramasser en somme) que certaines naïvetés, d'aucunes ingénuités de style pourraient heurter parfois nos préjugés d'écrivain visant à l'impeccable. La vérité de notre rectification éclatera dans le cours des citations que nous allons prodiguer . . .

Verlaine is as good as his word with regard to the final phrase since two-thirds of the remainder of the article is made up of quotations and precisely the same pattern is followed in the essay on Villiers de l'Isle Adam. As for the article on himself, this simply consists of four superficial pages of unimportant autobiographical information in the course of which Verlaine takes the opportunity of quoting two more poems by Rimbaud, 'Le Cœur volé' and 'Tête de Faune', that he had omitted from his article in the first series of *Poètes maudits*. In short, taking the six articles together, one cannot but agree with Jacques Borel that, 'à aucun moment ils n'ouvrent sur les œuvres des "poètes maudits" de profondes ou de secrètes perspectives'.[3]

One cannot but agree too with the same critic's similar judgement of the series of 'pot-boilers' that Verlaine, no doubt because of the success of *Les Poètes maudits*, was invited to contribute, between 1885 and 1893, to a collection called *Les Hommes d'aujourd'hui*. As the title suggests, these are brief portraits, about four pages long, of the leading literary figures of the day, and within so limited a space Verlaine could clearly say little of any real value. The formula he uses is very much the same as in *Les Poètes maudits*—a framework of biographical information filled in with an account of the literary work of the author concerned and sometimes accompanied by lengthy quotations. The article on Rimbaud, for example, again quotes the sonnet 'Voyelles' in full, again with little or no comment, and adds two further poems, the passages 'Aube' and 'Veillées' from the *Illuminations*, for which he simply expresses his admiration. The article on Mallarmé too, though whetting the public's appetite by including an unpublished poem—an early version of the sonnet 'Victorieusement fui le suicide beau'— gives little insight into the poet's ideas and technique, nor does the article on Heredia, although it quotes, with an enthusiasm which is perhaps surprising in one who had abandoned the Parnassian aesthetic, three of the sonnets which were later to be among the best-known poems of *Les Trophées*, 'Le Samouraï', 'Soir de Bataille' and 'Les Conquérants'. The choice of such poems may well be evidence of a sureness of taste on Verlaine's part, but it does not alter the fact that there is little or no attempt in *Les Hommes d'aujourd'hui* to rationalise this choice and to engage in serious critical studies either of the poets concerned or of the poems quoted.

Works of fiction

At the beginning of his career Verlaine had ideas about being a novelist and dramatist as well as a poet and critic. In 1867 he published in the magazine *Le Hanneton* a tale of mystery and horror entitled 'Le Poteau' obviously influenced by Edgar Allan Poe and in 1868, in collaboration with François Coppée, he published in the same magazine a playlet entitled 'Qui veut des merveilles?'. But, as with his criticism, these ventures into the novel and the drama proved to be false starts and it was not until 1886 that he produced a volume which included his short story of almost twenty years before and added to it two rather longer stories, 'Louise Leclercq' and 'Pierre Duchâtelet', each of about twenty pages, and a short, one-act playlet of half that length entitled 'Madame Aubin'. These three works all have a strongly autobiographical element—Louise Leclercq's flight from Paris to Brussels with her lover is clearly reminiscent of Verlaine's escapade with Rimbaud in 1872, although the ending to the story, with the two lovers living happily ever after, belongs to the realm of wishful thinking; the same is true of 'Madame Aubin', though with an alternative outcome equally far removed from harsh reality, since in this case the heroine repents of having run away with her lover and returns to her husband; as for 'Pierre Duchâtelet', in this tearful history of a brave young man volunteering to fight the enemy in 1870 and being abandoned by his faithless wife, we are no doubt meant to recognise, with the aid of rose-coloured spectacles, Paul Verlaine, all of whose troubles, he would have liked to think, stemmed from his selfless patriotism.

This brief account of these stories not only brings out their autobiographical element, it also gives some indication of their painful sentimentality. The characters are mere cardboard figures in whom it is impossible to believe, no doubt because Verlaine made no attempt to endow them with an independent existence but simply used them as thinly disguised versions of himself, so that the stories fall disastrously between two stools and are neither autobiography nor fiction. Instead they are simply shapeless little daydreams of what might have been.

In the same year that he published these prose works Verlaine published another volume with a somewhat misleading title, *Les Mémoires d'un Veuf*. These are not in fact memoirs at all but a collection of some forty prose poems, no doubt intended to rival, or at least to imitate in some degree, Baudelaire's *Petits Poèmes en Prose* and possibly even Rimbaud's *Illuminations* which were also published in 1886. Nearly all of them, however, had previously been published separately in various magazines, some as early as 1870, but the majority between 1882 and 1886. In a prefatory note to the volume Verlaine describes these passages gathered together 'sous un titre énorme' as being 'ni un petit roman, ni un recueil de minuscules nouvelles, mais bien des parcelles d'une chose vécue' and they are indeed, as he further admits in one of the passages entitled 'Apologie', of very diverse inspiration. Some are concerned with the details of his own life and have, on occasions, a directness which echoes to some slight extent that of Rimbaud, as in the final paragraph of 'Cheval de retour' with its evocation of Verlaine's tribulations on his return to Paris after the disastrous failure of his farming venture:

La nuit je grimpe mes cent marches à la lueur d'allumettes qui me brûlent le bout des doigts, avec de la fatigue plein les muscles, des chansons de la rue plein la tête; pour m'aller coucher et ne pas dormir au bruit jamais fini des fiacres aux stores baissés et des fardiers et des camions et des charrettes chargés de ferrailles, de meubles cassés et de boues.

On other occasions, however, they lapse into the embarrassing sentimentality of 'Pierre Duchâtelet', as in the passage 'A la mémoire de mon ami ***' which is a lament, not for Rimbaud, as one might have thought, or for Lucien Létinois, with whom Verlaine was still in contact at the time the passage was written in 1882, but for his schoolboy friend Lucien Viotti who had been killed in 1870:

A cette même table de café où nous avons causé si souvent face à face, après douze ans—et quelles années!—je viens m'asseoir et j'évoque ta chère présence. Sous le gaz criard et parmi le fracas infernal des voitures, tes yeux me luisent vaguement comme jadis, ta voix m'arrive grave et voilée comme la voix d'autrefois. Et tout ton être élégant et fin de vingt ans, ta tête charmante (celle de Marceau plus beau), les exquises proportions de ton corps d'éphèbe sous le costume de gentle-man, m'apparaît à travers mes larmes lentes à couler.

Hélas! ô délicatesse funeste, ô déplorable sacrifice sans exemple, ô moi imbécile de n'avoir pas compris à temps! Quand vint l'horrible guerre dont la patrie faillit périr, tu t'engageas, toi qu'exemptait ton cœur trop grand, tu mourus atrocement, glorieux enfant, à cause de moi qui ne valais pas une goutte de ton sang, et d'elle, et d'elle!

Other passages are literary essays, such as the obituary on Victor Hugo entitled 'Lui toujours—et assez' and the fairly lengthy study called 'Du Parnasse contemporain'. Others again are sketches for theatrical pieces, as is indicated by the titles 'Scénario pour ballet' and 'motif de pantomime', or descriptive passages about flowers, landscapes, cafés and so on.

But in none of the various and varied passages of *Les Mémoires d'un Veuf* can Verlaine be said to have achieved any real success. As Octave Nadal and Jacques Borel constantly and rightly emphasise, in their edition of the *Œuvres complètes*, Verlaine is uniquely, as they put it, a 'singer'. His particular and peculiar gift is for using words to form patterns of sound that powerfully reinforce the meaning of the words or even, on occasions, create a meaning for themselves. When Verlaine spurns his gift for melody he becomes the most ordinary and banal of writers. He entirely lacks Rimbaud's genius for accumulating scintillating images, or Baudelaire's skill at manipulating the flexible rhythms of prose in his *Petits Poèmes en Prose*. When Verlaine writes prose, it is quite simply prose, as in this paragraph from the passage 'Mal aria', written as early as 1870, which is like one of the landscapes of *Poèmes saturniens* with all the poetry removed:

Parlez-moi d'une après-midi de septembre, chaude et triste, épandant sa jaune mélancolie sur l'apathie fauve d'un paysage languissant de maturité. Parmi ce cadre laissez-moi évoquer la marche lente, recueillie, impériale, d'une convalescente qui a cessé d'être jeune depuis très peu d'années. Ses forces à peine revenues lui permettent néanmoins une courte promenade dans le parc: elle a une robe blanche, de grands yeux gris comme le ciel et cernés comme l'horizon, mais immensément pensifs et surchargés de passion intense.

It is perhaps significant that, two years after the publication of *Les Mémoires d'un Veuf*, Verlaine published, in the magazine *Le Décadent* in March 1888, the article in which he made his celebrated defence of rhyme: 'Rimez faiblement, assonez si vous voulez, mais rimez ou assonez, pas de vers français sans cela'.[4] It is true that what Verlaine was attacking was blank verse—'notre langue peu accentuée ne saurait admettre le vers blanc' he said elsewhere in the article—but it may be that he felt that much of the magic of his own style lay in his gift for finding simple, often tenuous, but none the less effective rhymes and that he had no talent either for blank verse or for prose.

Memoirs

Once Verlaine's fame, or notoriety, was firmly established, that is to say as from about 1890, he proved to be an inexhaustible mine of information, not always accurate, on his life and hard times. *Mes Hôpitaux* in 1891 and *Mes Prisons* in 1893 are the two best-known volumes of memoirs, but he also published, either in volume form, or in the form of instalments in magazines, or both, *Souvenirs* in 1891, *Souvenirs d'un Messin* in 1892, *Quinze Jours en Hollande* in 1893, *Confessions* in 1895 and various other items of the memoir kind. All were written in haste and as a means of making a little money in the easiest possible way. Some are of interest from a biographical point of view, provided the information can be checked against other sources, but none are of interest from the literary point of view. Jacques Borel describes the language of *Mes Prisons* in the following terms: 'Louche, surchargée, incorrecte souvent, elle témoigne, par rapport à la prose déjà fléchissante de *Mes Hôpitaux*, d'un recul considér-able'.[5] Even Antoine Adam admits a similar decline, though he is a little less ungenerous towards *Mes Hôpitaux*: 'Si, dans *Mes Hôpitaux*, la langue restait nette et ferme, on pouvait y remar-quer pourtant certaines phrases plus alambiquées que subtiles, des raccourcis excessifs, de l'obscurité. Ces défauts se multiplient dans le volume que donna l'écrivain en 1892 [*sic*] et qu'il intitula *Mes Prisons*'. M. Adam is prepared to forgive the innumerable errors of fact in *Mes Prisons* on the grounds that Verlaine's memory was failing, but what he finds less excusable is the way in which the language becomes disjointed and clumsy, and he quotes, in support of his complaint, the following typically involved phrase: 'Je ne saurais naturellement bien les préciser en ce moment de mon âge mûr, déjà!, après tant d'années et tant d'un peu plus sérieux verrous sur ma liberté d'homme, pour telles et telles causes, au nombre desquelles faut-il compter précisément l'abus de la conjugaison en question plus haut . . .'[6] As for *Confessions*, M. Adam points out that these were sold to their editor at a rate of 50 centimes per line and he uncharitably, but no doubt correctly, assumes that this is why Verlaine takes every opportunity to spin things out.[7] In the course of over two hundred pages he had only reached 1871 when the editor called a halt so that no later instalments of this leisurely autobiography exist.

Looking at Verlaine's prose work as a whole, a similar kind of pattern as in his poetry can be perceived, that is to say some promising early work in his critical articles on Baudelaire and Barbey d'Aurevilly and a vast amount of virtually worthless material turned out to order in the later years. What is lacking, however, in the prose work is the central core of mature work written during the half dozen years round about 1870 which exists in his poetry and without which Verlaine would be as forgotten as a poet as he deservedly is as a prose writer.

VII

VERLAINE AND HIS CRITICS

Critical opinion of Verlaine's work varied enormously throughout his career, not always in direct ratio to the quality of his poetry. A good example of this is provided by a review of *Poèmes saturniens* by Barbey d'Aurevilly who, in revenge perhaps for the scathing comments *Les Œuvres et les Hommes* had received the previous year, dismissed Verlaine as 'un Baudelaire puritain . . . sans le talent net de M. Baudelaire, avec des reflets de M. Hugo et d'Alfred de Musset ici et là. Tel est M. Paul Verlaine. Pas un zeste de plus'. He was of course right to recognise the influence of older writers in *Poèmes saturniens* but he was wrong to condemn the volume as being entirely derivative. His refusal, or inability, to recognise any original talent in *Poèmes saturniens* was so deep-rooted that he even quoted disparagingly the final line of 'Mon Rêve familier', one of the most successful poems in the volume, in order to make a cheap jibe at Verlaine: 'Il a dit quelque part, en parlant de je ne sais qui—cela du reste n'importe guère—"Elle a l'inflexion des voix chères qui se sont tues". Quand on écoute M. Verlaine, on désirerait qu'il n'eût jamais d'autre inflexion que celle-là'.[1]

Other critics, however, were more perceptive. Jules de Goncourt wrote to Verlaine: 'Merci pour vos vers. Ils rêvent et peignent. Mélancolies d'artistes ciselées par un poète . . . Vous avez ce vrai don: la rareté de l'idée et la ligne exquise des mots'.[2] Leconte de Lisle too recognised the technical skill that Verlaine had displayed: 'Vos *Poèmes* sont d'un vrai poète, d'un artiste très habile déjà et bientôt maître de l'expression'.[3] Banville and Sainte-Beuve both stressed the originality of *Poèmes saturniens*—'Vous visez à faire ce qui n'a pas été fait', said the latter, whilst the former wrote: 'Je suis certain que vous êtes un poète et que votre originalité est réelle'. In support of their compliments, unfortunately, both of them picked out poems which are by no means the best or the most original in *Poèmes saturniens*, Banville expressing a preference for the three rather trivial poems 'Femme et Chatte', 'Jésuitisme' and 'La Chanson des Ingénues' and Sainte-Beuve choosing two of the most clearly derivative poems in the whole volume, 'César Borgia' and 'La Mort de Philippe II'.[4] It may be, therefore, that their flattering comments should be taken with a grain of salt as simply the polite remarks inevitable in letters of thanks for the copies of his first volume of verse that Verlaine had sent them.

Nevertheless, *Poèmes saturniens* had attracted favourable attention in literary circles and Verlaine's feet seemed firmly set on the ladder leading to success. He took a further step up this ladder with the publication of *Fêtes galantes* in 1869 which brought from Victor Hugo the comment: 'Que de choses délicates et ingénieuses dans ce joli petit livre'.[5] *La Bonne Chanson*, however, had the misfortune to be printed just before the outbreak of the Franco-Prussian war in September 1870 and it was not published, in the sense of being made available to the public, until 1872 when hostilities had finally ended after the bitter civil strife of the Commune. By then Rimbaud had arrived in Paris and the relationship between him and Verlaine undoubtedly harmed the latter's reputation, particularly after July 1872 when the two poets left Paris to live together in London until the quarrel between them in July 1873. Verlaine's subsequent arrest and eighteen months' imprisonment in Belgium meant that he was still further ostracised as far as literary circles in Paris were concerned. As has been pointed out (see p. 90 above) he himself wrote, in a poem composed in prison in 1874:

> Las! je suis à l'Index et dans les dédicaces
> Me voici Paul V . . . pur et simple . . .

It is not therefore surprising that when *Romances sans Paroles* was published in March 1874 it was a disastrous failure and was completely ignored by the press and by the public. Eighteen months later, in October 1875, the poems Verlaine sent for inclusion in the third volume of *Le Parnasse Contemporain* were rejected by the editorial committee made up of Banville, Coppée and Anatole France. Since Verlaine had figured in the first two volumes in 1866 and 1869 this was a particularly cruel rebuff, and a particularly undeserved one as the admirable sonnet 'Beauté des femmes . . .', later included in *Sagesse*, is known to have been one of the poems submitted and the others probably included those written at the beginning of Verlaine's imprisonment, which are generally agreed to be among his finest work.[6] But this was not the view expressed by Anatole France who rejected the poems with the words: 'Non. L'auteur est indigne et les vers sont des plus mauvais qu'on ait vus'.[7]

Sagesse suffered the same fate as *Romances sans Paroles* when it was published in 1881. By then Verlaine had been away from Paris for almost ten years, so long a lapse of time that Zola, in an article which also appeared in 1881, referred to him as if he were dead: 'M. Verlaine, aujourd'hui disparu, avait débuté avec éclat par les *Poèmes saturniens*. Celui-là a été une victime de Baudelaire, et on dit même qu'il a poussé l'imitation pratique du maître jusqu'à gâter sa vie'.[8]

It was not until the following year, 1882, when Verlaine returned to Paris and began to mingle once again in literary circles that he started to re-establish his reputation as a poet. A major step in this process was the publication, in the magazine *Paris-Moderne*, of 'Art poétique', written eight years before and at first intended for the abandoned *Cellulairement* and then excluded from *Sagesse* because it did not fit in with the general tenor of this latter work. The young critic Charles Morice discussed the ideas put forward in 'Art poétique' in an article published in December 1882 in *La Nouvelle Rive Gauche* and from then on he became an ardent supporter of Verlaine, publishing the first critical study of him in 1888. By then, however, Verlaine's achievement had been recognised by others as well as Morice. In 1884 J. K. Huysmans had published his novel *A Rebours* which both reflected and moulded the tastes of the time. One of the chapters of the novel describes the literary preferences of its hero Floressas des Esseintes who has a particular affection for Flaubert, Edmond de Goncourt, Zola and Baudelaire, but who also admires a number of contemporary poets, among them Paul Verlaine. Through the intermediary of Des Esseintes Huysmans gives a perceptive and balanced judgement of Verlaine's work that deserves to be quoted at some length:

Paul Verlaine avait jadis débuté par un volume de vers, les *Poèmes saturniens*, un volume débile, où se coudoyaient des pastiches de Leconte de Lisle et des exercices de rhétorique romantique, mais où filtrait déjà, au travers de certaines pièces, telles que le sonnet intitulé 'Rêve familier', la réelle personnalité du poète . . . Puis, d'aucuns de ses livres, la *Bonne Chanson*, les *Fêtes galantes*, *Romances sans Paroles*, enfin son dernier volume, *Sagesse*, renfermaient des poèmes où l'écrivain original se révélait tranchant sur la multitude de ses confrères . . . Il avait pu exprimer de vagues et délicieuses confidences, à mi-voix, au crépuscule. Il avait pu laisser deviner certains au-delà troublants d'âme, des chuch- otements si bas de pensées, des aveux si murmurés, si interrompus, que l'oreille qui les percevait demeurait hésitante, coulant à l'âme des langueurs avivées par le mystère de ce souffle plus deviné que senti . . .[9]

After *A Rebours* Verlaine's reputation was secure and other writers and critics quickly followed in the footsteps of Morice and Huysmans. In 1885 Banville wrote, with regard to *Jadis et Naguère* which had just been published: 'Parfois vous côtoyez de si près le rivage de la poésie que vous risquez de tomber dans la musique. Il est possible que vous ayez raison',[10] an often quoted remark which admirably defines much of Verlaine's poetry, although it is less applicable to *Jadis et Naguère* than to earlier volumes. It was this musicality of Verlaine's poetry which was now constantly stressed. 'There are poems of Verlaine' wrote his English admirer, Arthur Symons, in 1899, 'which go as far as verse can go to become pure music'. But Symons also emphasised another feature of Verlaine's poetry: 'a simplicity of language which is the direct outcome of a simplicity of temperament'.[11] These two aspects of simplicity and musicality had already been noted in a striking way by one of the leading French critics of the day, Jules Lemaître, who said of Verlaine, in an essay first published in *La Revue Bleue* in January 1888 and included the following year in the fourth volume of a series entitled *Les Contemporains*: 'C'est un barbare, un sauvage, un enfant . . . seulement cet enfant a une musique dans l'âme et, à certains jours, il entend des voix que nul avant lui n'avait entendues'. Anatole France quoted this remark with approval in an article in *Le Temps* in 1890 (later published in *La Vie Littéraire* in 1899) and added: 'Il y a quelque chance qu'on dise un jour de lui ce qu'on dit aujourd'hui de François Villon auquel il faut bien le com- parer: "C'était le meilleur poète de son temps" '.[12]

But in thus making such lavish amends for his unnecessarily harsh rejection of the poems Verlaine had submitted to him some fifteen years before, Anatole France was perhaps being over-generous. The second half of the nineteenth century in France was particularly rich in poets and two of them, Rimbaud and Mallarmé, have a stronger claim than Verlaine to be considered as 'les meilleurs poètes de leur temps'.

In his Symbolist Manifesto published in *Le Figaro* on 18 September 1886 Jean Moréas had defined Verlaine's contribution to Symbolism as having been to 'briser les cruelles entraves du vers'. At that time it was no doubt true that Verlaine seemed to have done more than anyone to break the cruel bonds of versification, because Rimbaud's work was as yet scarcely known and was in fact not so much as mentioned by Moréas. But it is now apparent that Rimbaud went much farther than Verlaine in breaking away from traditional patterns of rhyme and rhythm. Verlaine's innovations were limited to a liking for the octosyllabic line rather than the alexandrine, the introduction, in a number of poems, of the 'vers impair', the extensive use of 'enjambement' and a preference for weak rather than rich rhymes. But Rimbaud, after following in the elder poet's footsteps for a brief period early in 1872, at the beginning of their relationship, soon overtook Verlaine as regards freedom of form and abandoned verse altogether in favour of prose poetry in his *Illuminations*. Similarly Mallarmé, after beginning as a Parnassian, like Verlaine, and then, again like him, moving towards a more evocative kind of poetry in *L'Après-midi d'un Faune*,[13] went far beyond any degree of freedom of form that Verlaine had attempted. In *Un Coup de Dés*, written in 1897, the year after Verlaine's death and the year before his own, Mallarmé used different kinds of lettering and distributed his words irregularly over the unit of the double page as part of his attempt to achieve the effect at which he was aiming in this highly original and complex work. And even in his apparently more conventional poems, such as the sonnets he wrote in the last ten years of his life, Mallarmé's twisted and tortured syntax, which enables him to give to his poems an extraordinary richness and density, makes Verlaine appear as a comparatively timid innovator.

As regards the content of their poetry too, there is no doubt that Rimbaud and Mallarmé, who were intellectually far superior to Verlaine, were pre-occupied with matters beyond the comprehension of 'pauvre Lélian'. In Rimbaud's *Une Saison en Enfer* 'la vierge folle' (who is, of course, Verlaine) says of l'époux infernal' (who is, of course, Rimbaud): 'J'étais sûre de ne jamais entrer dans son monde. A côté de son cher corps endormi, que d'heures des nuits j'ai veillé, cherchant pourquoi il voulait tant s'évader de la réalité'. To escape from reality into an ideal world, or rather to create an ideal world through the medium of poetry, was also the aim of Mallarmé who, according to Moréas, gave to Symbolism its 'sens du mystère et de l'ineffable'. Rimbaud and Mallarmé were therefore both Symbolists of the transcendental kind, endeavouring to penetrate beyond the superficial forms of the real world to the ideal forms of an infinite and eternal world. But Verlaine was a Symbolist of the human kind, concerned solely with the reflection of inner feelings in the objects of the outer world of reality. It is true that in some of the religious poems of *Sagesse* he conjures up a vision of an ideal world parallel with that conjured up by Rimbaud in his *Illuminations* or by Mallarmé in 'Prose pour des Esseintes', but precisely because this was a Christian and therefore traditional vision it lacked the novelty and the excitement of the ideal worlds towards which Rimbaud and Mallarmé aspired and had less appeal in an increasingly secular society.

Verlaine himself realised that he did not belong to Symbolism in its transcendental sense and in Jules Huret's *Enquête sur l'évolution littéraire* in 1891 he replied to the journalist's request for a definition of Symbolism in the following uninhibited passage, typical of his conversational style in his last years:

Vous savez, moi, j'ai du bon sens; je n'ai peut-être que cela, mais j'en ai. Le Symbolisme? . . . comprends pas . . . Ça doit être un mot allemand, hein? Qu'est-ce que cela peut bien vouloir dire? Moi, d'ailleurs, je m'en fiche. Quand je souffre, quand je jouis ou quand je pleure, je sais bien que cela n'est pas du symbole. Voyez-vous, toutes ces distinctions-là, c'est de l'allemandisme: qu'est-ce que cela peut faire à un poète ce que Kant, Schopenauer, Hegel et autres Boches pensent des sentiments humains! Moi, je suis Français, vous m'entendez bien, un chauvin de Français, avant tout. Je ne vois rien dans mon instinct qui me force à chercher le pourquoi du pourquoi de mes larmes; quand je suis malheureux, j'écris des vers tristes, c'est tout.

He also recognised, in the same article, that he did not share the advanced views on prosody of the younger generation of Symbolists:

> J'ai élargi la discipline du vers, et cela est bon; mais je ne l'ai pas supprimée! Pour qu'il y ait vers, il faut qu'il y ait rythme. A présent on fait des vers à mille pattes! Ça n'est plus des vers, c'est de la prose, quelquefois même ce n'est que du charabia.[14]

It was for these two reasons—the comparatively unadventurous nature of both the content and the form of his poetry, his inability to speculate on the 'pourquoi du pourquoi' of things and his reluctance to break completely with traditional forms of versification—that Verlaine's reputation, which had stood so high in his last years, soon suffered a steep decline. In February 1896, the month after his death, the magazine *La Plume* organised a second *enquête* parallel to the one Jules Huret had carried out half a dozen years before but this time centred on Verlaine, and already certain reservations were expressed. 'Il ouvrit la fenêtre' was the opinion of the eccentric *femme de lettres* Rachilde who had been a close friend of Verlaine's for many years.[15] Another close friend, Mallarmé, described Verlaine as having been caught up in 'le conflit de deux époques, une dont il s'extrait avec ingénuité, réticent devant l'autre qu'il suggère'.[16] A third contributor to the *enquête* however, Charles Maurras, was not content with veiled criticisms about Verlaine having merely opened windows, or having failed to complete the transition from one period to another; he expressed his view much more openly: 'Paul Verlaine laisse un grand nom; mais je ne sais s'il laisse une œuvre'.[17]

A few years later, with the arrival of Surrealism and the emphasis it laid both on the search for a world beyond reality and on total freedom of form, Verlaine's reputation sank still lower and André Breton, the leader of the Surrealists, for whom Rimbaud was the dominant figure of the earlier generation, stated categorically that 'la surestimation de Verlaine a été la grande erreur de l'époque symboliste'.[18]

Even an admirer of Verlaine such as Pierre Martino who, in 1924 wrote what is still probably the best study of the poet as a poet, agreed that Verlaine did not share the general ambition of the Symbolists to 'renouveler les thèmes poétiques et changer l'horizon même de la poésie' and that 'sa timidité dans le maniement des procédés nouveaux d'expression rhythmique, ses défiances à l'égard du vers libre tracent une espèce de ligne-frontière qui sépare très nettement son œuvre de celles qui eurent les préférences de la génération symboliste'.[19]

Thirty years later another Verlaine enthusiast, Antoine Adam conceded that, as far as the attitude of the public was concerned there was still 'une réticence que l'on sent générale',[20] and in 1955 A. M. Schmidt, in *La Littérature Symboliste*, revealed the extent to which he shared this reticence by hesitating to rank Verlaine alongside his fellow poets Mallarmé and Rimbaud and by finding a curiously non-committal adjective to describe his poetry: 'Moins grand sans doute que Mallarmé et Rimbaud . . . Verlaine a composé d'inimitables poèmes'.[21]

Yet although this view of Verlaine as a poet of the second rank as compared with his two great contemporaries is now generally accepted, it may well be that our continued admiration for the latter springs more from what they attempted than from what they achieved. Rimbaud's insistence that 'les inventions d'inconnu réclament des formes nouvelles' and Mallarmé's ceaseless struggle to find a means of expression that would enable him to create a non-existent world led both of them, in their different ways, 'aux limites extrêmes de la poésie', as R. Jasinski put it.[22] One could indeed go farther and claim that they went not merely to the extreme limits but even beyond the boundaries of poetry, for it now seems certain, after the vast amount of work that has been done on Rimbaud and Mallarmé over the last thirty years, that some of their work is destined to remain inaccessible even to the most perceptive and sympathetic reader.

It is when one turns away, perhaps with a certain impatience, from extreme originality of this kind, towards the poetry of Verlaine, that one wonders whether the latter's more modest achievements may perhaps stand the test of time better than the bolder attempts of his two contemporaries. 'Notre vingtième siècle, si intellectuel, est porté vers l'exégèse des œuvres où des problèmes d'interprétation se posent', wrote Eléonore Zimmermann in one of the most recent studies of Verlaine.[23] It may be that future years will adopt a different approach and will set greater store by Verlaine's unique gift for subtly conveying the infinite sadness of things. The heartsickness of hope deferred, the sense of lost youth, the suicidal loneliness of a rainy day, the fall of autumn leaves, the grief of separation, the stillness of moonlight, the melancholy of sunset, the dream that remains no more than a dream, simply the sadness of being sad—no one else has succeeded as well as Verlaine in re-creating these emotions in those who read his poetry.

NOTES AND REFERENCES

Details as to the publisher and date and place of publication of works listed in the bibliography are not repeated here.

I. THE BIOGRAPHICAL BACKGROUND

1. These two letters are quoted in Rimbaud, *Œuvres complètes*, Gallimard, Pléiade, 1963, pp. 281–5.

2. This letter is quoted in Mathilde Verlaine's *Mémoires de ma vie*, p. 210.

3. Rimbaud, *Œuvres complètes*, p. 290.

4. Ibid, p. 291.

5. Ibid, p. 297.

6. For the text of this 'acte de renonciation' see Rimbaud, *Œuvres complètes*, p. 306.

7. For a table setting out the details of Verlaine's spells in hospital from 1886–95 see Jean Richer, *Paul Verlaine*, pp. 78–9.

8. Y. G. Le Dantec in the 1948 edition of the *Œuvres poétiques complètes*, p. 1170.

II. THE EARLY POETRY

1. Compare Verlaine's lines with the first and last stanzas of Gautier's 'L'Art' published in the 1858 edition of *Emaux et Camées*:

> Oui, l'œuvre sort plus belle
> D'une forme au travail
> Rebelle,
> Vers, marbre, onyx, émail . . .
>
> Sculpte, lime, cisèle,
> Que ton rêve flottant
> Se scelle
> Dans le bloc résistant.

2. This is Jacques Borel's argument on p. 49 of the 1962 edition of the *Œuvres poétiques complètes*.

3. Edmond Lepelletier, *Paul Verlaine, sa vie, son œuvre*, p. 152.

4. J. H. Bornecque, *Les Poèmes saturniens de Verlaine*, pp. 90 ff.

5. The text of this preface to the second edition of the *Poèmes saturniens* can be found in Paul Verlaine, *Œuvres complètes*, II, p. 300.

6. For the latest information on the vexed question of the Lacaze Collection see Joanna Richardson, *Verlaine*, p. 31. Lepelletier's statement that the Galerie Lacaze in the Louvre had just been opened when Verlaine was writing *Fêtes galantes* was proved incorrect and both J. H. Bornecque and J. Robichez therefore assumed that Verlaine could not have seen the paintings concerned. Miss Richardson corrects this assumption by pointing out that the Lacaze Collection was exhibited elsewhere before its transfer to the Louvre. It is perhaps worth adding that in 1866 there was an exhibition in Paris of works by Fragonard and other minor eighteenth-century painters such as Nattier and Greuze (for a review of this exhibition see *La Revue des Deux Mondes*, vol. 63, 1866, pp 1053–60).

7. For further details on this point see M. Cutler, *Evocations of the XVIIIth century in French poetry, 1800–69*, Geneva, Droz, 1970, and E. Souffrin-Le Breton, 'Banville et la poétique du décor' in *French 19th century painting and literature*, edited by U. Finke, Manchester University Press, 1972.

8. J. H. Bornecque, *Lumières sur les 'Fêtes galantes'*, p. 167.

9. Edmond and Jules de Goncourt, *L'Art du XVIIIe siècle*, (première série) Paris, Fasquelle, 1918, p. 11.

10. Rimbaud, *Œuvres complètes*, p. 259.

11. See p. 139 of Jacques Borel's introduction to *La Bonne Chanson* in Verlaine, *Œuvres poétiques complètes*, 1962 edition.

12. See Antoine Adam, *Verlaine*, p. 91 and the English translation of this work by Carl Morse, *The Art of Paul Verlaine*, p. 87.

13. See Eléonore Zimmermann, *Magies de Verlaine*, p. 31.

III. THE MAJOR POETRY

1. See Antoine Adam, *Verlaine*, p. 93 and *The Art of Paul Verlaine*, p. 89.

2. Antoine Adam's statement, on the pages quoted in the preceding note, that Verlaine 'was alone in Paris from the second half of January to the middle of March' is a half-truth; he was alone in the sense that Mathilde was away, but Rimbaud was there and the two poets in fact lived together until Mathilde's return. In contrast with Adam another critic considers that 'given the circumstances of Verlaine's life at that moment, it is hard to see to whom the poet could be addressed if not to Rimbaud'. (See A. E. Carter, *Verlaine, a study in parallels*, p. 107.)

3. See, for example, A. E. Carter, op. cit., p. 108 and Eléonore Zimmermann, op. cit., p. 58.

4. See Antoine Adam, *Verlaine*, p. 93 and *The Art of Paul Verlaine*, p. 90.

5. See Jacques Borel in Verlaine, *Œuvres poétiques complètes*, 1962 edition, p. 179.

6. See Antoine Adam, *Verlaine*, pp. 97–8 and *The Art of Paul Verlaine*, pp. 93–4. M. Adam's attempt to link Verlaine with the Impressionists and to make of 'Walcourt' an Impressionist poem is unconvincing, not only because the poem is not purely and simply pictorial, but also because, although the beginnings of Impressionism were in the air as early as 1872, the Impressionist technique of juxtaposing dabs of paint of different colours, which M. Adam suggests Verlaine is practising in 'Walcourt', was known only to the small circle of painters led by Monet, until the celebrated exhibition of 1874 as a result of which the term 'Impressionism' was created.

7. Is this the same landscape as in 'Dans l'interminable / Ennui de la plaine', but seen in summer instead of winter? Eléonore Zimmermann, op. cit., p. 304, notes that not only is 'la plaine immense' reminiscent of 'l'interminable ennui de la plaine' but that an earlier line 'ce Sahara de prairies' seems to echo 'la neige incertaine luit comme du sable'. If this is so then Adam's hypothesis that 'Dans l'interminable . . .' was written at Paliseul in the Ardennes at Christmas 1871, is no longer tenable. But on the other hand it may well have been written in early April 1873 when Verlaine returned from London to Jehonville via Ostend, travelling from west to east across the lowlands of Belgium that he had crossed from south to north in the summer of the preceding year when he had written 'Malines'. In a letter written in the middle of May from the family farm near Charleville Rimbaud states that 'il gèle le matin' suggesting a long cold spring when 'la neige incertaine' may well have still been lying on the flat plains of Belgium in early April.

8. Y. G. Le Dantec in the 1948 edition of the *Œuvres poétiques complètes*, p. 921.

9. Jacques Borel in the 1962 edition of the *Œuvres poétiques complètes*, p. 186.

10. For further details on this point see C. Chadwick, 'Two obscure sonnets by Verlaine', *Modern Language Review*, vol. 52, 1957, p. 349 and *Etudes sur Rimbaud*, Nizet, 1959, p. 50. See also Eléonore Zimmermann, op. cit., pp. 244–7.

11. See V. P. Underwood, *Verlaine en Angleterre*, p. 104.

12. In an article in *French Studies*, April 1971, on 'Verlaine's "Beams" ', D. D. R. Owen suggests, as a remote possibility, identifying 'elle' with the boat. But he dismisses the idea at once, preferring to see 'elle' as Rimbaud, with religious undertones of Christ walking on the water.

13. See P. Martino, *Verlaine*, p. 110.

14. For further details on this point see C. Chadwick, *Etudes sur Rimbaud*, pp. 49–59.

15. For the probable date of 'Dans l'interminable / Ennui de la plaine' see note 7 to Chapter III above.

16. These remarks apply only to the first fourteen lines of 'La bise se rue . . .', since the final six lines were added later and alter the sense of the poem giving it a religious significance.

17. See the letter dated 'Jehonville, le 19 mai '73' in Paul Verlaine, *Correspondance*, I, p. 101.

18. For details on the date of 'L'espoir luit . . .' see C. Chadwick, 'Two obscure sonnets by Verlaine', *Modern Language Review*, vol. 52, 1957, pp. 350–4. See also Verlaine, *Sagesse*, edited by C. Chadwick, The Athlone Press, 1973, pp. 91–2.

19. J. Robichez, *Verlaine*, *Œuvres poétiques*, p. 604.

20. Stéphane Mallarmé, *Avant-dire au 'Traité du verbe' de René Ghil*, 1886, see *Œuvres complètes*, Gallimard, Pléiade, 1948, p. 857.

21. On a number of occasions Verlaine places a word of two or more syllables in the centre of the line, spanning the place where the caesura normally falls, in the way that Rimbaud had noted in 'Dans la Grotte' in *Fêtes galantes* (see p. 28 above), as in the following examples:

Puis franchement et simplement viens à ma Table . . .

Et que sonnent les Angélus roses et noirs
En attendant l'assomption dans ma lumière . . .

Et l'extase perpétuelle de la science . . .

D'une joie extraordinaire, votre voix . . .

22. For a commentary on this sonnet, found in Rimbaud's wallet by the Brussels police in July 1873 and in all probability written in May 1873 rather than May 1872, see C. Chadwick, 'Two obscure sonnets by Verlaine', *Modern Language Review*, vol. 52, 1957, pp. 347–50.

IV. THE MINOR POETRY

1. 'Ah! vraiment c'est triste . . .' is one of the four poems 'faits ici récemment' which Verlaine sent to Lepelletier in an undated letter probably written from the Prison des Petits Carmes in Brussels just before his transfer to the prison at Mons on 25 October, judging by his remark, 'jusqu'à nouvel ordre ne m'écris plus, je suis tellement sur le provisoire maintenant'. It should be noted that this letter is misplaced in Ad. van Bever's edition of Verlaine's *Correspondance*, I, p. 126, but its date is correctly deduced by the editors of the *Œuvres complètes*, II, p. 1062.

2. See Y.-G. Le Dantec in Verlaine, *Œuvres poétique complètes*, 1948 edition, pp. 979-80.

3. Antoine Adam, *Verlaine*, p. 136.

V. THE LAST POEMS

1. Edmond Lepelletier, op. cit., p. 524.

2. P. Martino, op. cit., p. 142.

3. Y. G. Le Dantec, *Verlaine, Œuvres poétiques complètes*, 1948 edition, p. 1053.

4. Antoine Adam, *Verlaine*, pp. 150-2.

5. Ibid., pp. 138-40.

6. Ibid., pp. 144-7.

7. Jacques Borel, *Verlaine, Œuvres complètes*, II, p. 24.

8. Ibid., p. 988.

9. Ibid., pp. 329-30.

10. Ibid., pp. 334-6.

11. Antoine Adam, *Verlaine*, p. 146.

12. Jacques Borel, *Verlaine, Œuvres complètes*, II, p. 577.

13. Ibid., p. 578.

14. A. E. Carter, op. cit., pp. 222-5.

15. Joanna Richardson, op. cit., p. 238.

16. Is it significant that Verlaine cannot even quote his own poems correctly? The line in inverted commas is from 'A la Promenade' in *Fêtes galantes* but it should read: 'Et le vent doux ride l'humble bassin'.

17. Joanna Richardson, op. cit., p. 239.

18. Ibid., p. 335.

19. Ibid., p. 278.

20. Ibid., p. 292.

21. Ibid., p. 289.

22. Ibid., p. 309.

23. Antoine Adam, *Verlaine*, p. 138.

24. Ibid., p. 139.

25. See L. Morice, *Verlaine, le drame religieux*, pp. 419-22.

VI. THE PROSE WORKS

1. The fact that Verlaine expresses the same ideas in criticism as in poetry seems to disprove Jacques Borel's suggestion (see note 2, Chapter II, above) that the 'Epilogue' of *Poèmes saturniens* is 'une parodie délibérée et secrètement ironique, s'inscrivant finalement contre l'esthétique à laquelle de tels poèmes semblent souscrire'.

2. Verlaine's quotation from Baudelaire's essay on Théophile Gautier

is not quite correct. Baudelaire actually wrote 'un enlèvement de l'âme', not 'une excitation à l'âme', and 'la passion est chose naturelle', not 'la passion est naturelle'.

3. Verlaine, *Œuvres complètes*, I, p. 444.
4. Ibid., vol. I, p. 895.
5. Ibid., vol. II, p. 575.
6. Antoine Adam, *Verlaine*, p. 150.
7. Ibid., p. 160.

VII. VERLAINE AND HIS CRITICS

1. Barbey d'Aurevilly's review is quoted in Charles Donos, *Verlaine intime*, pp. 31–2.
2. Ibid., pp. 32–3.
3. Ibid., p. 33.
4. Ibid., pp. 33–5.
5. Ibid., p. 58.
6. See Paul Verlaine, *Correspondance*, II, pp. 3–6, letters to Emile Blémont dated 6 September, 20 September and 27 September 1875. It is the second of these letters that asks Blémont to add 'Beauté des femmes . . .' to the 'petit paquet parnassien' which, according to the first letter, Verlaine had sent him more than two months before.
7. Michel Corday, *Anatole France*, Flammarion, 1927, p. 137.
8. This article was reprinted in Emile Zola, *Documents littéraires*, Paris, Bibliothèque Charpentier, 1891, under the title *Les Poètes contemporains*. The comment on Verlaine appears on p. 178.
9. J. K. Huysmans, *A Rebours*, Editions Fasquelle, 1968, pp. 229–30.
10. Banville's letter is quoted in Charles Donos, op. cit., pp. 118–19.
11. Arthur Symons, *The Symbolist movement in literature*, Heinemann, 1899, p. 89.
12. Anatole France, *La Vie Littéraire*, vol. 3, Calmann-Lévy, 1899, p. 317.
13. In 1891 Mallarmé said of Verlaine: 'C'est lui qui a le premier réagi contre l'impeccabilité et l'impassibilité parnassiennes; il a apporté, dans *Sagesse* [*sic*], son vers fluide avec, déjà, des dissonances voulues. Plus tard, vers 1875, mon *Après-midi d'un faune* fit hurler le Parnasse tout entier . . . J'y essayais, en effet, de mettre, à côté de l'alexandrin dans toute sa tenue, une sorte de jeu courant pianoté autour, comme qui dirait d'un accompagnement musical fait par le poète lui-même . . .' (Mallarmé, *Œuvres complètes*, Gallimard, Pléiade, 1948, p. 870). Mallarmé is clearly mistaken in referring to *Sagesse* as being before 1875 and he must have meant one of the earlier volumes, no doubt *Poèmes saturniens* or *Fêtes galantes*.

14. Jules Huret, *Enquête sur l'évolution littéraire*, pp. 67–9.

15. Pierre Martino, op. cit., p. 201.

16. Mallarmé, *Œuvres complètes*, Gallimard, Pléiade, 1948, pp. 873-4.

17. Pierre Martino, op. cit., p. 201.

18. Breton's remark is quoted by J. R. Lawler, *The Language of French Symbolism*, Princeton, U.P., 1969, p. 32.

19. Pierre Martino, op. cit., p. 184.

20. A. Adam, *Verlaine*, p. 168.

21. A. M. Schmidt, *La Littérature Symboliste*, p. 29.

22. R. Jasinski, *Histoire de la littérature française*, Boivin, 1947, vo l. 2, p. 681.

23. Eléonore Zimmermann, op. cit., p. 11.

SELECT BIBLIOGRAPHY

EDITIONS

Paul Verlaine, *Œuvres complètes* (2 vols.), introduction d'Octave Nadal, études et notes de Jacques Borel, texte établi par H. de Bouillane de Lacoste et Jacques Borel, Le Club du meilleur livre, 1959–60.

Paul Verlaine, *Œuvres poétiques complètes*, texte établi et annoté par Y.-G. Le Dantec, édition révisée, complétée et présentée par Jacques Borel, Gallimard, Bibliothèque de la Pléiade, 1962.

Paul Verlaine, *Œuvres en prose complètes*, texte établi, présenté et annoté par Jacques Borel, Gallimard, Bibliothèque de la Pléiade, 1972.

Paul Verlaine, *Œuvres poétiques*, édition de Jacques Robichez, Garnier, 1969.

Paul Verlaine, *Correspondance* (3 vols.), édition d'Ad. van Bever, Messein, 1922–9.

CRITICISM

Antoine Adam, *Verlaine*, Hatier-Boivin, 1953 (latest edition 1965), translated into English as *The Art of Paul Verlaine*, New York, University Press, 1963.

J. H. Bornecque, *Les Poèmes saturniens de Paul Verlaine*, Nizet, 1952.

J. H. Bornecque, *Lumières sur les Fêtes galantes*, Nizet, 1959.

J. H. Bornecque, *Verlaine par lui-même*, Editions du Seuil, 1966.

A. E. Carter, *Verlaine, a Study in Parallels*, Toronto, University Press, 1969.

Claude Cuénot, *Le Style de Paul Verlaine*, Centre de Documentation Universitaire, 1963.

Charles Donos, *Verlaine intime*, Vanier, 1898.

Jules Huret, *Enquête sur l'Évolution littéraire*, Bibliothèque Charpentier, 1891.

Edmond Lepelletier, *Paul Verlaine, sa vie, son œuvre*, Mercure de France, 1907.

Pierre Martino, *Verlaine*, Boivin, 1924 (new and revised edition 1951).

Charles Morice, *Verlaine*, Vanier, 1888.

Louis Morice, *Verlaine, le Drame religieux*, Beauchesne, 1946.

Octave Nadal, *Verlaine*, Mercure de France, 1961.

François Porché, *Verlaine tel qu'il fut*, Flammarion, 1933.

Jean-Pierre Richard, 'Fadeur de Verlaine' in *Poésie et Profondeur,* Editions du Seuil, 1955.

Joanna Richardson, *Verlaine*, Weidenfeld and Nicolson, 1971.

Jean Richer, *Paul Verlaine*, Seghers, 1960.

V. P. Underwood, *Verlaine et l'Angleterre*, Nizet, 1956.

Ex-Mme. Paul Verlaine, *Mémoires de ma vie*, Flammarion, 1935.

Georges Zayed, *La Formation littéraire de Paul Verlaine*, Geneva, Droz, 1962.

Eléonore Zimmermann, *Magies de Verlaine*, Corti, 1967.

INDEX